Spotlight on Shakespeare

A practical introduction
Sandy Brownjohn and Gareth Gwyn-Jones

To Andrew Steeds, for his good humour and
editorial integrity in times of adversity.

Acknowledgments

The Publishers would like to thank the following for permission to use
copyright illustrations:

Page 6t, 6b, Jarrold Publishing; p 7, Shakespeare Centre Library,
Stratford-upon-Avon; p 9, Shakespeare Centre Library, Stratford-upon-
Avon; p 10, Fotomas Index; p 11t, 11b, Mary Evans Picture Library;
p 12, Guildhall Library, London; p 13, Jarrold Publishing; p 14, by
permission of the trustees of the British Museum; p 16, Mander and
Mitchenson Theatre Collection; p 20t, 20b, Dulwich Picture Gallery;
p 21t, 21m, Dulwich Picture Gallery; p 21b, Shakespeare Centre
Library, Stratford-upon-Avon; p 22l, Mary Evans Picture Library;
p 22r, Fotomas Index; p 24, Shakespeare Centre Library, Stratford-upon-
Avon; p 25t, Robert Harding Picture Library/Corpus Christi College,
Cambridge; p 25b, The Mansell Collection; p 26t, Fotomas Index;
p 26b, Private Collection; p 27l, Private Collection; p 27r, National
Portrait Gallery; p 28, National Portrait Gallery; p 32b, Jarrold
Publishing; p 32t, Public Record Office; p 47, Carol Walkin RE/Mullet
Press; p52, Mary Evans Picture Library; p 58, The Mansell Collection.
All other photographs by Sandy Brownjohn and Roy Matthews.

British Library Cataloguing in Publication Data
Brownjohn, Sandy
   Spotlight on Shakespeare.
   I. Title   II. Gwyn-Jones, Gareth
   822.3

ISBN 0 340 52846 X

First published 1992

Typeset by Litho Link Ltd, Welshpool, Powys.
Printed in Italy for the educational publishing division of Hodder
& Stoughton Ltd, Mill Road, Dunton Green, Sevenoaks, Kent by
New Interlitho S.P.A., Milan.

Contents

Shakespeare's Plays

● ● ● ● ● ●

Comedies
(including tragicomedies)

The Two Gentlemen of Verona
The Taming of the Shrew
The Comedy of Errors
Love's Labour's Lost
A Midsummer Night's Dream
The Merchant of Venice
The Merry Wives of Windsor
Much Ado About Nothing
As You Like It
Twelfth Night
Troilus and Cressida
Measure for Measure
All's Well That Ends Well
Pericles, Prince of Tyre
The Winter's Tale
Cymbeline
The Tempest
The Two Noble Kinsmen

Tragedies

Titus Andronicus
Romeo and Juliet
Julius Caesar
Hamlet
Othello
Timon of Athens
King Lear
Macbeth
Antony and Cleopatra
Coriolanus

Histories

Henry VI, Part 1
Henry VI, Part 2
Henry VI, Part 3
Richard III
Richard II
King John
Henry IV, Part 1
Henry IV, Part 2
Henry V
Henry VIII

Shakespeare and
Elizabethan Theatre

● ● ● ● ● ●

'This blessed plot, this earth, this realm, this England.' (Richard II)

● ● ● ● ● ●

William Shakespeare 1564-1616

It is generally accepted that William Shakespeare was the author, or co-author, of 38 plays which have survived to this day. We also know that he wrote others which have not survived, but we will probably never know how many. He also wrote many poems in sonnet form.

His early life – the facts

There are many stories about the boyhood of Shakespeare, most of which have simply been made up. We know very few facts about his early life – the rest we have to guess.

On 23 April 1564, St George's Day, William Shakespeare was born, probably in a house in Henley Street, Stratford-upon-Avon. His mother, Mary, was the daughter of Robert

Shakespeare's birthplace, Stratford-upon-Avon

'. . . a star danced, and under that I was born.' (Much Ado About Nothing)

Arden, a member of an old and well-known Warwickshire family. William's father, John, was a successful glovemaker and became an important figure in Stratford. He owned two houses in Henley Street. Four years after William was born, John was made High Bailiff (Mayor) of Stratford which meant that he was also a Justice of the Peace (a magistrate).

In spite of this, John Shakespeare himself ended up in court on several occasions for minor offences. In 1559 he, with others, had been fined four pence by the council 'for not kepyinge ther gutteres clene'.

In 1596, this coat of arms was granted to Shakespeare's father. The spear on it is a play on the name Shakespeare. The motto at the top means 'Not without right'.

William's baptism was recorded in the parish list or 'register' of Holy Trinity Church, Stratford, on 26 April 1564, in Latin:
'Gulielmus filius Johannes Shakspere'
(William son of John Shakespeare)

In 1578, John Shakespeare had to borrow £40, a large sum of money at that time. The document dealing with the loan includes the name of William Shakespeare; this is the first official mention since his baptism.

There is also a document asking for a special licence to marry Anne Hathaway; this is the third and final official record of these years. Anne was the daughter of a farmer from Shottery, near Stratford. William was 18 and Anne was 26; in those days this was almost past the age when she could have hoped to marry. The special licence suggests they

'It is a wise father that knows his own child.' (The Merchant of Venice)

needed to marry in a hurry, probably because Anne was pregnant. Six months after the wedding, their first child, Susanna, was born, followed two years later by the twins, Judith and Hamnet.

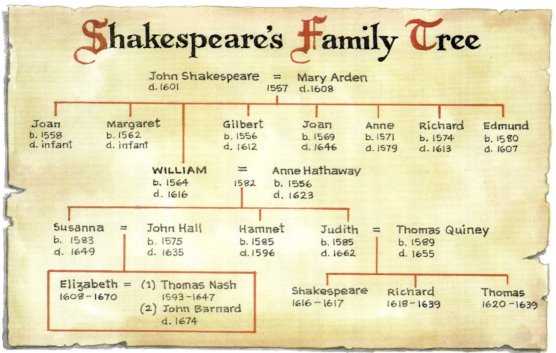

Shakespeare's Family Tree

John Shakespeare = Mary Arden
d. 1601   1557 d.1608

Joan
b. 1558
d. infant

Margaret
b. 1562
d. infant

Gilbert
b. 1556
d. 1612

Joan
b. 1569
d. 1646

Anne
b. 1571
d. 1579

Richard
b. 1574
d. 1613

Edmund
b. 1580
d. 1607

WILLIAM = Anne Hathaway
b. 1564   1582 b. 1556
d. 1616   d. 1623

Susanna = John Hall
b. 1583   b. 1575
d. 1649   d. 1635

Hamnet
b. 1585
d.1596

Judith = Thomas Quiney
b. 1585   b. 1589
d. 1662   d. 1655

Elizabeth = (1) Thomas Nash
1608–1670   1593–1647
          (2) John Barnard
                  d. 1674

Shakespeare
1616 – 1617

Richard
1618 –1639

Thomas
1620 –1639

Shortly after, possibly in 1585, William left his home and his family. Exactly when, where and why he went, we can only guess. All we know is that there is a reference to an actor and writer in London in a book called 'Greene's Groatsworth of Wit', dated 1592, which is thought to be Shakespeare. But where had he been for seven years since leaving Stratford?

HOW TO SPELL SHAKESPEARE'S NAME

It was only in the eighteenth century that people began to follow fixed, or 'standard', ways of spelling words. In Shakespeare's day, people just spelt words as they thought they sounded. Shakespeare's name has been written in many different ways, including the following:

Shakspeyr	Shaxpeare	Shagspere
Shagsper	Shakspere	Shaxper
Shaxpere	Shakeshaft	Shakesper

In fact, over 80 versions have appeared at one time or another.

'My salad days/When I was green in judgement' (Antony and Cleopatra)

His early life – conjecture

Much of Shakespeare's early life still remains a mystery. There are not even any records to prove whether he went to school. However, it is likely that William went to Stratford Grammar School, which was only a few minutes walk from his home in Henley Street.

There have been many suggestions as to why Shakespeare left his wife and family. One popular idea was that he had been caught poaching deer from Sir Thomas Lucy's estate and had run away to avoid being whipped or imprisoned. However, for a number of reasons, this is very unlikely. People have said that Shakespeare must have been, at various times, a teacher, lawyer, soldier, sailor, preacher, a minder of horses outside theatres and a butcher. He certainly knew about many occupations, but did he gain this knowledge simply by travelling widely and talking to many people? Did he, in fact, leave home to join a touring company of actors?

We will never know for certain when and how Shakespeare established himself in London's theatre world. All we can say is that at some time between 1585 and 1592, when his name was first mentioned in Greene's publication, William Shakespeare took up the career of actor and writer.

King Edward VI Grammar School, Stratford-upon-Avon: Shakespeare was probably a pupil at this school.

● ● ● ● ● ●

Bankside

During the reigns of Elizabeth I and James I, a number of theatres were built on the south bank of the Thames, near London Bridge, in an area known as Bankside. There were already arenas here for bear-baiting and bull-baiting, and for centuries Bankside had had a reputation for gambling, drinking and low life.

Wrongdoers on Bankside might well end up in the local Clink prison. This is where the slang term for prison comes from ('being in clink'!). Also nearby was the Marshalsea Prison, the most important prison after the Tower of London.

Between 1587 and 1599, three theatres – the Rose, the Swan and the Globe – were built on Bankside. The Bear Garden was converted to become the Hope Theatre in 1614.

'We have seen better days' (Timon of Athens)

Real bear gardens

The bull- and bear-baiting rings near the Globe were popular places of entertainment. Londoners would flock to see these 'sports' where dogs were set onto a bull or bear which was chained to a stake. Sometimes the bear was torn to pieces, but often it was the dogs that died, or that were wounded along with their quarry. Even Queen Elizabeth enjoyed watching this spectacle. This cruel pastime has long since been banned, and we may now find it difficult to understand its appeal. For Elizabethans, however, it was a good day out. They also enjoyed a public execution and people fought to get a ringside seat to watch a prisoner being beheaded. Traitors' heads were stuck on poles over the southern Bridge Gate of London Bridge.

Other entertainments

Elizabethans played a number of sports. At Court they might play 'real' tennis (different from today's game) which is still played occasionally at Hampton Court. They also went hawking and hunting (each noble family kept falcons and hawks) and enjoyed jousting. The common people often played bowls, a kind of hockey with curved sticks, or football, the most popular game of all. The football was an inflated pig's bladder. In those days, whole villages might play, and games were rowdy, without rules or fair play, and they frequently ended in riots and arrests.

'Many a good hanging prevents a bad marriage.' (Twelfth Night)

● ● ● ● ● ●

A visit to the theatre in Shakespeare's day

If you went to an Elizabethan theatre to see a play, it would have been rather like going to a football match today. The streets would have been full of hurrying people; a noisy crowd, laughing and jostling, buying food and trinkets from street sellers along the way. Posters and handbills would be seen advertising the day's programme. Flying high above the theatre would be the theatre company's flag, showing that a performance was going to be given that day. The city streets would be jammed with carriages if the performance was at the Fortune or the Blackfriars; if it was at the Globe or the Rose, south of the river on Bankside, you would have to cross a crowded London Bridge or hire one of the small river ferries, while trumpet blasts sounded from the theatre towers to hurry the people along.

Bankside performances were always in the afternoon because there was no artificial lighting and the audiences needed to get home by nightfall. It cost 1d (1 penny) to stand in the pit, 2d to sit in the galleries, and 3d for a private box, and there could be over 2000 people in the audience. There were no tickets or reserved seats, but 'Gatherers' collected the money at the entrance. The money was then put into a box which was locked away in an office during the performance. This is where the term Box Office originated.

At 2 o'clock three trumpet blasts were given, to show that the play was about to begin, but there was none of the respectful silence that would be expected today. Throughout the play, sellers moved among the audience, selling fruit, nuts, wine and beer, cards, tobacco and playbooks. Not surprisingly, there were often pickpockets and thieves at work too. People would carry on talking, eating and drinking during the play, and if they did not like what they saw they were quite likely to hiss, boo or throw fruit at the actors. Shakespeare's plays, however, would probably escape this treatment as they were very popular. Shakespeare provided his audiences with all they could ask for: laughter, romance, good plots, villains and heroes, and, very often, violence and bloody murder.

One of the things that would strike us now about the Elizabethan theatre would be the smell. Shakespeare himself, in *Julius Caesar*, mentions the smell of the crowds, their sweaty bodies and stinking breath. These were mixed with the smells of food and drink, the smoke from tobacco (recently introduced by Sir Walter Raleigh), and the overpowering stink of garlic, used by people both as a medicine and as protection against witchcraft and evil spirits. If there were any toilets, these were open buckets, which did not help to improve the atmosphere!

As a playgoer you would have been able to see a different play almost every day. Companies kept large numbers of plays in their repertoire, which they put on in rotation. In London the law allowed companies to perform every day of the year, except Sundays, but in practice this did not happen. Theatres sometimes had to close because of bad weather or for some religious festival. London theatres were also closed six times between 1592 and 1610 because of outbreaks of the plague which could spread disastrously in the crowded conditions of the theatre.

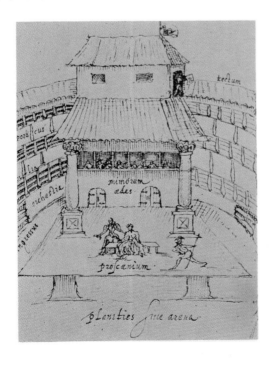

The interior of the Swan playhouse (Johannes de Witt, 1596).

● ● ● ● ● ●

London theatres

There were two types of theatre in London. Amphitheatres were similar in design to innyards and bear-baiting rings, and were open to the skies. Halls had roofs and were smaller, with more expensive seats. They were often lit by as many as 150 candles for each performance.

An engraving of London by Claus Visscher: the Bear Garden and the Globe are in the foreground.

The amphitheatres

The Red Lion
This was the first theatre specially built for the sole purpose of putting on plays.

The Globe
Shakespeare's company of actors was called the Lord Chamberlain's Men. The actors had their own theatre known simply as the Theatre at Shoreditch. When the lease ran out on the Theatre, they had to find a new home. The Theatre had been built like a construction kit, so the actors were able to take it apart, carry the timbers across the river and rebuild it as the Globe.

The Globe had many sides, with galleries on three levels around an open yard. Its thatched roof covered only the galleries. Because it was not protected from the weather, the Globe was only open in the summer months and was closed from October to April.

Audiences at the Globe were large, even by today's standards. It is said that 2,500 people might be in the theatre at one time.

The first performance at the Globe was given by Shakespeare's company, the Lord Chamberlain's Men, in 1599. Over the next thirteen years, Shakespeare regularly performed there both in his own plays and in those by Ben Jonson, who was another famous writer.

On 30 June, 1613, during a performance of Shakespeare's play, *Henry VIII*, a stage cannon was fired to announce the entrance of King Henry. A spark from the cannon set fire to the thatched roof and in one hour the Globe had been burned to the ground. Fortunately, no one was killed – though one man did have his breeches set alight! Personal disaster was averted when he put the flames out with a bottle of ale. When the Globe was rebuilt, the thatched roof was replaced with tiles.

The Rose
The Rose was the first Bankside theatre. It was built in 1587 by Philip Henslowe and became the home of the Lord Admiral's Men, led by the most celebrated actor of the day,

Edward Alleyn. The Rose, however, could not compete with the Globe and in 1600 Henslowe and Alleyn moved their company across the river to the new Fortune Theatre. The final performance at the Rose took place two years later.

The Swan and The Hope

These two theatres, at different times, provided Bankside competition for the Globe. The Lord Chamberlain's Men also appeared at the Swan which was built just four years before the Globe. However, the Swan lost its popularity after some of its actors, including Ben Jonson, were sent to the Marshalsea prison for performing a play which the authorities thought was offensive.

The Hope was built by Philip Henslowe in 1614. It had originally been the Bear Garden and still provided bear-baiting on two days a week, with plays on the other four. However, bear-baiting proved more popular than plays and soon became its main function.

The halls

The Blackfriars

Of all the hall playhouses the Blackfriars was the most important.

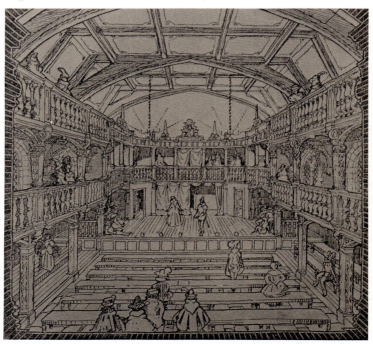

Interior of the Blackfriars

In 1596, James Burbage had paid £600 for this chamber, which had once seen the trial of Catherine of Aragon, Henry VIII's first wife. Burbage had converted it to a theatre but died long before permission was given for his company to perform there. If permission had been granted earlier, and Shakespeare's company had been able to use the theatre, the Globe would probably never have been built. The King's Men, formerly called the Lord Chamberlain's Men, appeared at the Blackfriars for the first time in 1609 in front of an all-seated audience. Thereafter, the Blackfriars became the home of the King's Men in the winter months when the Globe was closed.

The Blackfriars was smaller than the Globe, and the seats were more expensive, ranging from sixpence to half a crown (30 old pennies). By 1630, the Blackfriars was more important than the Globe.

The Blackfriars was finally closed in 1642, as were all theatres after the English Civil War, because the new Puritan government disapproved of them. It was demolished in 1665.

● ● ● ● ● ●

The actor in Shakespeare's day

Although there were several hundred actors in Shakespeare's day, few of them achieved lasting fame. Indeed, until actors became members of reputable companies such as the King's Men, they were still regarded as vagabonds who were not to be trusted.

Even the 'respectable' actors had a reputation for causing trouble. One of them, Gabriel Spenser, was killed by Ben Jonson in a duel. Jonson was lucky to escape the hangman's rope – his only punishment was to have his thumb branded.

Becoming an actor

Most actors joined companies as young apprentices. If they were older, they were hired to play small parts. Boy actors whose voices had not yet broken played female roles, because women were not permitted to act.

The parts an actor had to learn were handwritten on strips of parchment. He would also be given the cue speeches (the lines directly before his own speeches) of other actors, but never the whole play. An actor needed to be able to read well and would therefore have had to have received some education. This meant that he was likely to come from a middle-class family.

A successful actor needed considerable skills. In any one week, he might act in six different plays and perform several different characters in each play. But he needed more than just an excellent memory; he had to be able to dance, sing, play an instrument, fence, and be generally fit and athletic in order to play the sorts of parts that Elizabethan audiences demanded.

Casting and rehearsals

A new play would be rehearsed for about three weeks before a company would be ready to perform it. Rehearsals always took place in the mornings; performances began at 2 o'clock in the afternoon.

1. Machinery for lowering actors to the stage
2. Storage
3. The 'Heavens'
4. Pulley system
5. Balcony
6. Props room
7. Dressing room and wardrobe
8. Back stage (the tiring house)
9. Props
10. Stage trap door
11. The 'Hell'

'To be or not to be: that is the question . . .' (Hamlet)

King James I (1566–1625)

Companies changed plays frequently, sometimes performing as many as six in a week, with some being shown once only. Actors, therefore, had no time to develop characters because they had so many lines to learn from so many different plays. This meant that they were usually typecast. In other words, they always played the same sort of character. In the Lord Chamberlain's company, William Shakespeare usually played kings and noblemen, Will Kempe was the company comedian or clown, while Richard Burbage always played the leading role. To do this in play after play, Burbage would have had to learn hundreds of words every day, as well as rehearse and perform – an enormous task.

The company used very little in the way of scenery and props. For instance, a forest would be indicated by a bush placed in a barrel. If an actor wore a cloak, the audience knew it was an outdoor scene; if he carried a lantern or a candle it was night-time. With so many plays, it was not practical to have complicated sets. In any case, the actors might, on occasions, have to go straight from the afternoon performance of one play at the Globe or the Blackfriars to Court for an evening performance by candlelight of a different play.

These Court performances often took place at the royal palaces of Whitehall or Greenwich and were paid for by Queen Elizabeth and, later, King James. Shakespeare's company regularly performed in front of royalty and, after James came to the throne, made more Court appearances than all the other companies put together.

The leading actors

Edward Alleyn (1566–1626)

Alleyn was the leading actor of his time and was famous for his great voice and his enormous energy on stage. He was a leading member of Lord Strange's Men, who later became the Lord Admiral's Men, managed by Philip Henslowe. On marrying his first wife, Henslowe's step-daughter, he became Henslowe's partner, managing and acting with the Admiral's Men at the Rose Theatre. He helped Henslowe build the Fortune Theatre and eventually became the owner of both theatres. He gave up acting altogether in 1604 to concentrate on management.

Edward Alleyn (1566–1626)

'O! This learning, what a thing it is!' (The Taming of the Shrew)

Richard Burbage (1567–1619)

Richard Burbage was the son of James Burbage who built the Theatre. Richard Burbage was Alleyn's greatest rival. He and his brother, Cuthbert, began as child actors in their father's theatre, the Theatre. With his brother and five other actors, including Shakespeare and Will Kempe, he built the Globe using the timbers of the Theatre. From 1595 to 1618, Burbage was leading actor and manager for the Lord Chamberlain's Men and the King's Men at the Theatre, the Globe and the Blackfriars. He was excellent in tragic roles, and Shakespeare wrote many of his tragic characters for him. He was the first actor to play Hamlet, Macbeth, King Lear, Richard III and Othello. He was also a talented oil painter. He was born three years after William Shakespeare and died three years after him in 1619.

Richard Burbage (1567–1619)

Nathan Field (1587–1620)

Field was an actor and minor playwright who started out in a boys' company. His chief claim to fame is probably that he replaced Shakespeare in the King's Men in 1615; many people, however, thought that he was second only to Burbage as a leading actor. He wrote two plays of his own and collaborated on others with fellow writers such as Fletcher.

Nathan Field (1587–1620)

Other important actors

When the Lord Chamberlain's company was formed, eight of the actors in the company became part-owners. These were Richard Burbage, Shakespeare, Kempe, John Heminges, Augustine Phillips, George Bryan, William Sly and Thomas Pope. Henry Condell took over Bryan's share after Bryan's death. In the same way, a number of people owned the Globe and the Blackfriars. Richard and Cuthbert Burbage each owned a quarter of the Globe, and the rest was divided between Shakespeare, Kempe, Heminges, Pope and Phillips. The actors sharing the Blackfriars were Shakespeare, Heminges, Sly and Condell.

Without Heminges and Condell much of Shakespeare's work would probably have been lost, for, when Richard Burbage died, they were the only two members of the original Lord Chamberlain's company left alive. They

Enter Lady.
La. That which hath made them drunk, hath made me bold:
What hath quench'd them, hath giuen me fire.
Hearke, peace: it was the Owle that shriek'd,
The fatall Bell-man, which giues the stern'st good-night.
He is about it, the Doores are open:
And the surfeted Groomes doe mock their charge
With Snores. I haue drugg'd their Possets,
That Death and Nature doe contend about them,
Whether they liue, or dye.
Enter Macbeth.
Macb. Who's there? what hoa?
Lady. Alack, I am afraid they haue awak'd,
And 'tis not done: th'attempt, and not the deed,
Confounds vs: hearke: I lay'd their Daggers ready,
He could not misse 'em. Had he not resembled
My Father as he slept, I had don't.
My Husband?
Macb. I haue done the deed:
Didst thou not heare a noyse?
Lady. I heard the Owle schreame, and the Crickets cry.
Did not you speake?
Macb. When?
Lady. Now.

A page from the first folio of Shakespeare's works, published in 1623. John Heminges and Henry Condell were largely responsible for Shakespeare's plays surviving to the present day.

'Men of few words are the best men.' (Henry V)

gathered together all Shakespeare's plays, many of which had not been printed. Heminges, who had been financial manager of the King's Men, died in 1634, the wealthiest of all the company, owning a quarter of both the Globe and the Blackfriars.

John Lowin, who joined the King's Men in 1603, outlived all his former colleagues. He was a large, jolly man who made his name playing such parts as Falstaff and Henry VIII. In 1649, seven years after the Puritans closed all the theatres, Lowin was punished for acting in secret performances at the Cockpit.

The leading comic actors

Richard Tarleton (?–1588)

Tarleton was the most famous and popular of the Elizabethan comic actors and was the first great stage clown. He was short and fat, with a large face and curly hair, a flat nose and a squint, and a moustache and beard. Audiences recognised him at once and enjoyed him hugely. He could sing and dance, and he would quite often ignore scripts and put in his own lines and jokes as he went along. So, in many ways, today's 'stand-up' comedians are following this tradition. Tarleton was a founder member of the Queen's Men in 1583, but died in poverty in 1588.

Richard Tarleton (?–1588)

Will Kempe (?-1603)

Kempe succeeded Tarleton in the Queen's Men and went on to become the leading comedian in the Lord Chamberlain's Men in plays by both Shakespeare and Ben Jonson. He was part owner (10 per cent) of the Globe but left the Lord Chamberlain's Men in 1599 and gave up his share of the theatre. He later toured Europe with acting companies and also worked for the Earl of Worcester's Men at the Rose Theatre. He followed in Tarleton's footsteps as the most famous clown in London and, like Tarleton, was known for his baggy breeches – a style copied by many of today's clowns. His habit, which he also shared with Tarleton, of making up his own lines did not please Shakespeare and may have explained why Kempe left the company. Kempe was famous for dancing a Morris dance from London to Norwich in nine days in 1600.

Will Kempe (?-1603), dancing to Norwich

'Lord, what fools these mortals be!' (A Midsummer Night's Dream)

The theatre companies

The Lord Chamberlain's Men (later known as the King's Men)

The Lord Chamberlain's Men was formed in 1594, in order to provide Court entertainment. It was one of two companies licensed to perform in London. Richard Burbage ran the company, and Shakespeare and Ben Jonson were resident actors and playwrights. We only have evidence to prove that Shakespeare belonged to the Lord Chamberlain's Men, but he probably worked with other companies too.

The Lord Chamberlain's Men performed at the Theatre, the Curtain, the Swan, the Cross Keys and the Globe and on more than 100 occasions before Queen Elizabeth.

The King's Men

In 1603, James I became King. Within six weeks he had taken over the Lord Chamberlain's Men and given them the new title of the King's Men. The company performed mainly at the Globe, or from 1609, at the Blackfriars; they also toured the country. The King's Men played at Court more than all the other companies put together.

The Lord Admiral's Men

Like the Lord Chamberlain's Men, the Lord Admiral's Men was formed in 1594, at the end of a plague epidemic. It was headed by Edward Alleyn, Richard Burbage's great rival. The company performed mainly at the Rose, but transferred to the new Fortune Theatre soon after the Lord Chamberlain's Men opened at the Globe.

'Some men are born great, some achieve greatness, and some have greatness thrust upon them.'
(Henry IV, Part I)

● ● ● ● ● ●

Shakespeare's fellow writers

Elizabethan England was the beginning of a new era in theatre. One reason for this was that there were permanent theatre buildings for the first time ever. Another was that plays began to appear in print (although not all the printed versions are reliable). Many were dictated from memory by actors or play-goers who wanted to earn money quickly. But at least many plays that would have been lost in previous years survived.

How plays were written

Nearly all the playwrights of the Elizabethan theatre met and discussed their work with fellow writers. Shakespeare was part of a group of writers who met to drink, dine and discuss at the Mermaid Tavern near St Paul's on the first Friday of each month. Most, at some time, collaborated with others so that plays were often the result of team work.

Plays were generally written for particular actors in the various companies, often in a very short time. Shakespeare might still have been working on a play while the completed part was being learned and rehearsed. It was quite usual for friends to supply ideas, lines or whole scenes for a play that was urgently required. It was also usual for actors to want to alter lines of new plays during rehearsals – they still do this today! Few plays can have reached the audience in the form the writer intended and solely as his own composition.

'This above all: to thine own self be true . . .' (Hamlet)

Christopher Marlowe (1564–1593)

Marlowe was born in the same year as Shakespeare. He was famous for the heroic characters he wrote for Edward Alleyn to perform. Marlowe was the principal writer for the Rose theatre, but he also collaborated with others, quite possibly with Shakespeare on *Titus Andronicus* and *Henry VI.*

Marlowe was often in trouble with the law and was arrested on a number of occasions, most seriously on a charge of murder. He spent 13 days in Newgate prison and was then set free. At the age of only 29 he was himself stabbed to death in a tavern brawl. There were rumours that he had been assassinated because he had been spying for the government.

The death of Christopher Marlowe in a tavern brawl.

'Brevity is the sole of wit.' (Hamlet)

Thomas Kyd (1558–1594)

Kyd was six years older than Marlowe. He was another successful Elizabethan playwright whose work must have influenced Shakespeare. Kyd set a fashion for tragic themes of blood and vengeance and was the author of the most popular of all Elizabethan tragedies, *The Spanish Tragedy*. This play was performed regularly up to 1642, when all the theatres were closed during the Civil War.

Ben Jonson (1572-1637)

Jonson was a leading member of a group of Elizabethan dramatists. After leaving Westminster School he was, for a time, a bricklayer and a soldier before he became an actor with Philip Henslowe's company in 1597. He was not very successful as an actor, but he soon started writing plays for the Admiral's Men, first in a team with three other playwrights and then on his own. He also wrote and acted for the Lord Chamberlain's Men and performed in early Globe productions of both Shakespeare's and his own plays. Unlike Shakespeare, Jonson took great pains to have his plays printed and preserved.

He was a close friend of Shakespeare and a regular drinking companion at the Mermaid Tavern. Jonson easily lost his temper and, like Marlowe, was often in trouble with the law and went to prison several times. His crimes ranged from writing material the authorities found offensive, to being in debt. He also narrowly escaped hanging for killing Gabriel Spenser, a fellow actor. In 1605, Jonson and two fellow writers, George Chapman and John Marston, made flippant references to Scots in their play *Eastward Ho!*. Since King James was a Scot, this was not a wise move. They were all imprisoned.

Despite his clashes with authority, Jonson wrote more Court Masques than any other writer. King James granted him a pension and Jonson became, unofficially, the first Poet Laureate. On his death he was buried in Westminster Abbey.

Ben Jonson (1572–1637)

'The quality of mercy is not strained.' (The Merchant of Venice)

Sir Francis Beaumont (1584–1616)

Together with John Fletcher, Beaumont was one of the great names of a later group of writers of the age, often writing as a member of a team. He worked very closely with Jonson and also collaborated with Fletcher, with whom he shared rooms. They wrote together for the King's Men, but in 1613 Beaumont married into a wealthy family and gave up writing entirely. Three years later he died, aged only 32.

John Fletcher (1579–1625)

Fletcher's name is always linked with Beaumont's but he collaborated with other writers too. He is thought to have worked with Shakespeare on *Henry VIII*, *Two Noble Kinsmen* and another play, *Cardenio*, which has been lost. With Beaumont, he wrote first for the boy-actors at the Blackfriars, and was then engaged to replace Shakespeare as principal dramatist for the King's Men. He died of the plague in 1625.

Sir Francis Beaumont (1584–1616)

John Fletcher (1579–1625)

Make-up in Elizabethan times

*Queen Elizabeth I
(1533–1603)*

The use of make-up became more widespread when Elizabeth I came to the throne as all the ladies of Court tried to copy her appearance. Portraits of Elizabeth show her to have red hair (known as Royal Auburn), a high forehead, white skin, red lips, thin eyebrows and white teeth. The truth, however, was different.

Elizabeth was bald in her later years and had to wear a wig. Her face was plastered with a white paste, her eyebrows were plucked and her teeth yellow, rotting and, in places, missing altogether, particularly on the left. Ladies who tried to look like her ended up looking just as bad, or even dying in the attempt!

Beauty spots or patching
Women often stuck small black plasters made of taffeta or felt on their faces to highlight features. Sometimes there were so many that these looked like ' . . . gnats or fleas of every imaginable shape and size'.

'I would not be a queen/For all the world.' (Henry VIII)

The grave consequences of wanting to look like the Queen

Beware – Poison!

Hair was dyed red with henna but often had to be bleached first with HYDROGEN PEROXIDE (quicklime) which eventually made it fall out. When that happened, wigs had to be worn. To achieve a high forehead, the hair was shaved back and eyebrows were plucked.

Eyes had to be sparkling and preferably blue. The juice of the plant BELLADONNA was used as eyedrops to create this effect. In Italian 'belladonna' means 'beautiful woman'; but the English name for the plant is Deadly Nightshade. Prolonged use could cause blindness.

Faces had to be white. A paste made from tallow (animal fat) and POWDERED LEAD was plastered on and glazed with egg white. This set hard and made it difficult for the person to smile or eat. The lead ate into the skin making holes.

Lips were painted with a deep red dye containing MERCURY so whenever people licked their lips they swallowed a little mercury. In time, many became ill or died from the build-up of the mercury in their stomachs.

Cheeks were painted with rouge made from MERCURIC SULPHIDE which, when breathed in through the nose, could add to the mercury in the stomach.

Teeth were not cleaned often. On the few occasions when they were, people might use soot and coal, or sometimes even pumice (volcanic rock). This was like using sandpaper and it wore off the enamel, so the teeth went bad and rotted away.

'I am dying, Egypt, dying.' (Antony and Cleopatra)

Perfume

People did not wash very often, so they used perfume to mask the smell. Both men and women soaked their clothes and themselves in perfume and carried pomanders (sweet smelling herbs or spices). They might not wash their hands for a week, but they would continue to eat with one hand and blow the nose with the other! Germs thrived through lack of hygiene.

The Elizabethan Court would smell disgusting to us. Strong perfumes would have mingled with the atmosphere of body smells, bad breath and rancid animal fat. A woman's beauty could be shortlived. Before long she might be bald, almost blind, her face pockmarked, her mouth full of blackish, yellowish stumps, her lips sore and her stomach full of mercury. Make-up could be a deadly business; indeed, many people thought it was the work of the Devil.

HOW TO COLOUR THE HEAD OR BEARD INTO A CHESTNUT COLOUR IN HALFE AN HOUR (Hugh Plat 1602)

Take one part of lead calcined with Sulphur, and one part of quicklime: temper them somewhat thin with water: lay it upon the hair, chafing it well in, and let it dry one quarter of an hour or thereabouts; then wash the same off with fair water divers times: and lastly with sope and water, and it will be a very natural hair-colour. The longer it lyeth upon the haire, the browner it groweth. This coloureth not the flesh at all, and yet it lasteth very long in the hair.

'All the perfumes of Arabia will not sweeten this little hand.' (Macbeth)

Shakespeare's last years

In June 1613, *Henry VIII*, the play Shakespeare probably wrote with John Fletcher, was being performed at the Globe. Unfortunately, one of the stage cannons used during the performance shot some burning paper onto the thatched roof. The fire spread and the whole wooden theatre was burned to the ground. Sir Henry Wotton was present at the disaster and wrote about it in a letter dated 2 July, 1613. After describing how the thatch caught fire, he went on to say:

'This was the fatal period of that virtuous fabric, wherein yet nothing did perish but wood and straw, and a few forsaken cloaks; only one man had his breeches set on fire, that would perhaps have broiled him, if he had not by the benefit of a provident wit put it out with bottle-ale.'

The Globe was rebuilt with a tiled roof but it was following this event that Shakespeare sold his share in the theatre and returned to Stratford. He still visited London quite often, but he now spent more and more time in Stratford with his family. In 1616 he made his will, and then revised it in March of the same year after the marriage of his daughter, Judith. The following month, probably on his birthday, 23 April, 1616, he died, aged fifty-two.

In his will, William left Judith a large sum of money and his broad silver-gilt bowl. His other daughter, Susanna, received most of his goods and property, including New Place, the finest house in Stratford, which Shakespeare had bought in 1597. To his sister, Joan, he left £20 which was roughly equal to what a man might earn in a year. He also left her all his clothes, and the Henley Street house for life. His wife, Anne, under English law, automatically received a third of his estate and was mentioned in the will in this famous line:

'I give unto my wife my second best bed.'

This was a very common bequest in wills as it referred to the marriage bed. The best bed was usually reserved for guests.

'Nothing in his life/Became him like the leaving it.' (Macbeth)

To friends in Stratford, and to his London friends from The King's Men, John Heminges, Richard Burbage and Henry Condell, he left 26 shillings and 8 pence (26s.8d) each, to buy memorial rings. This was a normal practice and the rings were worn in memory of the dead friend.

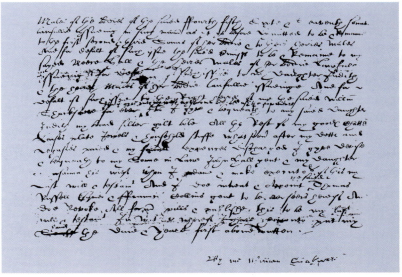

The final page of Shakespeare's will

Shakespeare was buried on 25 April, 1616, in Holy Trinity Church, Stratford. On his grave the epitaph runs:

> 'Good friend, for Jesus' sake forebear
> To dig the dust enclosed here;
> Blessed be the man that spares these stones
> And cursed be he that moves my bones.'

Shakespeare's grave in Stratford-upon-Avon

A monument was commissioned from Geerart Janssen (Gerard Johnson), a stonemason who worked near the Globe in London. The painted bust is near Shakespeare's grave in Stratford which people from all over the world visit. But it is his plays, finally collected and published after his death by his friends, Heminges and Condell, which have become Shakespeare's most lasting memorial.

*'. . . Nature might stand up
And say to all the world, "This was a man!"'*
(Julius Caesar)

The Plays

• • • • • •

'. . . All the world's a stage
And all the men and women merely players:
They have their exits and their entrances;
And one man in his time plays many parts.'
(As You Like It)

Romeo and Juliet

● ● ● ● ● ●

THE SOURCE OF THE PLAY

The story of Romeo and Juliet is an ancient one, and there have been many translations from the original Greek into Italian, French and English. Shakespeare took the story, developed the characters and created his own play. It has become one of the great love stories of all time.

ROMEO AND JULIET

Romeo and Juliet has inspired several composers. Tchaikovsky and Prokofiev, both Russian, composed music which is used for the ballet, *Romeo and Juliet.* In more modern times, the twentieth century American composer, Leonard Bernstein, wrote the musical *West Side Story*, which is based on the story of Romeo and Juliet.

'Parting is such sweet sorrow.' (Romeo and Juliet)

THE CHARACTERS

PROLOGUE:

Two households, both alike in dignity,
    In fair Verona, where we lay our scene,
From ancient grudge break to new mutiny,
    Where civil blood makes civil hands unclean.
From forth the fatal loins of these two foes
    A pair of star-crossed lovers take their life:
Whose misadventur'd piteous overthrows
    Do with their death bury their parents' strife.

● ROMEO

Romeo is the son of Montague, who is Capulet's enemy. He is young, around 17, and is infatuated with Rosaline at the beginning of the play. At the Capulets' ball he falls in love with Juliet, whom he later marries in secret. When he kills her cousin, Tybalt, in revenge for his friend, Mercutio, matters become worse. He is banished, but returns on hearing that Juliet is dead. Challenged by Paris, he kills him and then commits suicide next to Juliet in her tomb.

● JULIET

Juliet is the daughter of Lord Capulet, Montague's enemy. She is young, around 14, and has led a very quiet life. She falls in love with Romeo and secretly marries him. After he is banished, her parents arrange her marriage with Paris, a nobleman. To avoid marrying Paris she takes a potion that makes her appear dead. Romeo, seeing her in her tomb, thinks she really is dead and kills himself; when she wakes up, she too commits suicide to be with him.

● MERCUTIO (Mer-cue-she-o)

Mercutio is a friend of Romeo and a relation of the Prince of Verona. This likeable character is a young man who loves to joke and have a good time. He is loyal to Romeo and cannot bear to hear Tybalt insulting his friend. He fights Tybalt but is killed when Romeo accidentally distracts him when trying to break up the fight.

● BENVOLIO – Romeo's cousin

Benvolio is a sensible, peaceful young man who persuades Romeo to go to the Capulets' ball, hoping that Romeo will meet a girl to take his mind off Rosaline for whom he is 'lovesick'. Benvolio is a peacemaker, but he is still unable to prevent the fight which leads to the deaths of Mercutio and Tybalt.

● FRIAR LAURENCE – A Franciscan monk

Friar Laurence is a wise and holy priest who is a friend to both families. He agrees to marry Romeo and Juliet because he realises they are really in love, and he hopes this will bring an end to the feud between the families. It does, but not in the way he had hoped. His messenger fails to reach Romeo with news that Juliet is not really dead. Their double suicide is what finally brings the two families together.

● *PARIS – a noble relation of the Prince*

Paris is a kind and honourable man whose marriage to Juliet has been arranged by her parents. Devastated by her 'death', he mourns outside her tomb and challenges Romeo on his arrival there. Romeo, not knowing who it is, kills him in self-defence. Paris is another tragic victim of the feud between the families.

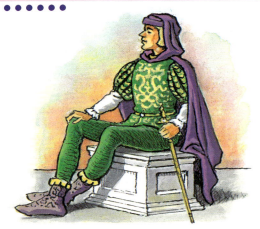

● *TYBALT (Tib-all-t) – Juliet's cousin*

Tybalt is an arrogant young man who is quick-tempered and hates the Montagues. He is an excellent swordsman and is generally played as a nasty character. He would have killed Romeo at the ball if he had not been restrained. The next day, burning to avenge Romeo's insult to his family, he goes looking for a fight. Romeo refuses to fight but Mercutio challenges Tybalt and is killed by him. Romeo then kills Tybalt in return.

● *THE NURSE – to Juliet*

The Nurse is a simple, motherly character who has looked after Juliet from the cradle. She is not very clever and fusses over Juliet. She helps Juliet in her secret marriage to Romeo, but she later urges her to marry Paris: this way she loses Juliet's confidence.

WHAT'S IN A NAME?

TYBALT is a version of TYBERT (or Tibert) who is the King of the Cats in an old fable called *Reynard the Fox*. This explains Mercutio's words in the scene on page 41: 'Tybalt, you rat-catcher, will you walk?' and: 'Good king of cats, nothing but one of your nine lives'. *Reynard* was a well-known and popular story, and Tybert is probably the origin of favourite pet cat names like Mr Tibs and Tibbles.

*'What's in a name? that which we call a rose
By any other name would smell as sweet.'* (Romeo and Juliet)

THE PLOT

For many years there has been bitter quarrelling between the two leading families of Verona, the Montagues and the Capulets. This leads to fighting whenever servants or members of the two families meet. Eventually, the Prince of Verona orders that any such fighting will be punishable by death.

Romeo thinks he loves a girl called Rosaline, but she does not return his love. Benvolio and Mercutio tease him about her and suggest that they all go to the Capulets' ball where he might meet someone else and then forget about Rosaline. They go in disguise, wearing masks, something which was quite common at such gatherings.

At the ball, Tybalt recognises Romeo's voice. He feels his family has been insulted by Romeo's presence and swears to have his revenge. Romeo meets Juliet and they immediately fall in love. Only later do they realise each other's identity, but by then it is too late to change their feelings.

At midnight, Romeo climbs into the Capulets' garden. Standing below the balcony of Juliet's bedroom, he overhears her say that she is in love with him. Both of them are well aware of the problems of falling in love with 'the enemy', but nevertheless, they decide on a secret marriage the next day.

Friar Laurence agrees to perform the marriage ceremony, but on the same day there is trouble when Tybalt, who is now related to Romeo by marriage, meets Benvolio and Mercutio in the street. Romeo tries unsuccessfully to stop them fighting, and Tybalt kills Mercutio. Anger then overcomes Romeo who avenges his friend by killing Tybalt.

The Prince decides not to sentence Romeo to death, but banishes him for ever from Verona for his part in the fight. Before leaving for Mantua the next morning, Romeo spends the night secretly with Juliet at the Capulet home.

Juliet's father, not knowing anything about her marriage to Romeo, now arranges a marriage for her with a nobleman called Paris. Since she cannot tell anyone that she is already married, she turns to Friar Laurence for help. He gives her a potion which she must swallow on the eve of her wedding to Paris. This medicine will make her seem dead for two days. Her body will then be taken to the family vault, from where Romeo can rescue her when she awakes. Friar Laurence promises to get word to Romeo to tell him the plan.

Unfortunately, the Friar's message does not reach Romeo, who only hears that Juliet is dead. Heartbroken, he buys some poison and hurries to Verona intending to die in the vault by her side. Outside the vault he is challenged by Paris. They fight and Romeo kills him. Then Romeo prises open Juliet's tomb and drinks the poison.

Almost immediately, Juliet awakes, expecting to find Romeo there. When she sees his dead body, she tries to drink the poison too, but there is none left. She then takes Romeo's dagger from his belt and stabs herself, to die by his side.

The Prince, Lord Montague and Lord Capulet are called to the tomb where the feuding families are reconciled: rather than being united by the marriage of the two young lovers, they are drawn together by grief at their deaths.

A FIGHT SCENE
ACT 3 SCENE 1 (abridged)

(a public place)

Characters: MERCUTIO, BENVOLIO, TYBALT, ROMEO, attendants.

BENVOLIO: I pray thee, good Mercutio, let's retire:
The day is hot, the Capulets abroad,
And, if we meet, we shall not 'scape a brawl.
By my head, here come the Capulets!

MERCUTIO: By my heel, I care not!

(Enter TYBALT, *with attendants)*

TYBALT: Follow me close, for I will speak to them. Gentlemen, good-den: a word with one of you.

MERCUTIO: And but one word with one of us? Couple it with something; make it a word and a blow.

TYBALT: You shall find me apt enough to that, sir, an you will give me occasion.

MERCUTIO: Could you not take some occasion without giving?

TYBALT: Mercutio, thou consort'st with Romeo, –

MERCUTIO: Consort! what, dost thou make us minstrels? An thou make minstrels of us, look to hear nothing but discords: here's my fiddlestick; *(indicates his sword)* here's that shall make you dance.

BENVOLIO: We talk here in the public haunt of men:
Either withdraw unto some private place,
And reason coldly of your grievances,
Or else depart; here all eyes gaze on us.

MERCUTIO: Men's eyes were made to look, and let them gaze;
I will not budge for no man's pleasure, I.

TYBALT: Well, peace be with you, sir. Here comes my man.

(Enter ROMEO)

TYBALT: Romeo, the hate I bear thee can afford
No better term than this, – Thou art a villain.

ROMEO: Tybalt, the reason that I have to love thee
           Doth much excuse the appertaining rage
           To such a greeting. Villain am I none;
           Therefore, farewell; I see thou know'st me not.

TYBALT: Boy, this shall not excuse the injuries
           That thou hast done me; therefore turn and draw.

ROMEO: I do protest I never injur'd thee;
           But love thee better than thou can'st devise
           Till thou shalt know the reason of my love:
           And so, good Capulet, – which name I tender
           As dearly as my own – be satisfied.

MERCUTIO: O calm, dishonourable, vile submission!

                        (*draws sword*)

           Tybalt, you rat-catcher, will you walk?

TYBALT: What wouldst thou have with me?

MERCUTIO: Good king of cats, nothing but one of your nine lives. Will you pluck your
           sword out of his pilcher by the ears? Make haste, lest mine be about your
           ears ere it be out.

TYBALT: I am for you. (*draws sword*)

ROMEO: Gentle Mercutio, put thy rapier up.

MERCUTIO: Come, sir, your passado. (*they fight*)

ROMEO: Draw, Benvolio; beat down their weapons.
           Gentlemen, for shame, forbear this outrage!
           Tybalt, – Mercutio, – the Prince expressly hath
           Forbidden bandying in Verona streets.
           Hold, Tybalt! – good Mercutio.

(MERCUTIO *is hit by* TYBALT's *sword and* TYBALT *runs off, followed by his attendants*)

MERCUTIO: I am hurt; –
           Where is my page? – go, villain, fetch a surgeon.
           A plague on both your houses!
           Why the devil came you between us? I was hurt under your arm.

ROMEO: I thought all for the best.

MERCUTIO: Help me into some house, Benvolio,
           Or I shall faint. – A plague on both your houses!
           They have made worm's meat of me.

STAGE SWORD FIGHTING

The best swords for this are plastic rapiers with rubber safety tips (available from toyshops).

● *ATTACK*

I Aiming for the left shoulder

2 Aiming for the right shoulder

3 Aiming for the left thigh

4 Aiming for the right thigh

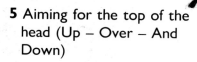

5 Aiming for the top of the head (Up – Over – And Down)

● *DEFENCE (PARRY)*

I Point your sword straight upwards. Push your opponent's sword away to the side and down, so that it points to the ground in the finish.

2 Similar move – 'back-handed' – with your arm going in the opposite direction.

3 Point your sword straight down (back of your hand facing your opponent's sword) and push the other sword aside.

4 Similar move – pushing the sword away to the right.

5 Raise your sword horizontally above your head to stop your opponent's sword, which is coming from above.

'If you prick us, do we not bleed?' (The Merchant of Venice)

ON GUARD – FEET AT 90° (TO START)

SHOULDER ATTACK AND PARRY

ATTACK TO LEFT SHOULDER

ATTACK TO HEAD

THIGH ATTACK AND PARRY

ATTACK TO LEFT THIGH

THE LUNGE

HEAD ATTACK AND PARRY

Watches, of course, should never be worn during a performance.

A Midsummer Night's Dream

● ● ● ● ● ●

THE SOURCE OF THE PLAY

Shakespeare created this play himself, unlike many of his other works which were loosely based on fact or other stories. The story of Theseus and Hippolyta by the Greek writer Plutarch had been translated into English in the sixteenth century. Into this tale, Shakespeare wove the fairy kingdom of Oberon, a character taken from an old French play, and Titania, another name for the goddess Diana. Puck's name comes from an old word 'pouk' meaning 'little devil'. For the tradesmen of Athens, Shakespeare mainly drew on his knowledge of ordinary country folk like those he would have known in the area around Stratford.

The 'play within the play', the story of Pyramus and Thisbe, had been translated from Latin and had been well known since the Middle Ages. Shakespeare's audiences would have recognised it immediately. This tragic story has some similarities with *Romeo and Juliet*, where misunderstandings cause the death of both lovers in that story too.

A MIDSUMMER NIGHT'S DREAM

A Midsummer Night's Dream has inspired two popular operas. One is by the nineteenth-century German composer, Felix Mendelssohn, which he wrote when he was 17 years old. The other is by the twentieth-century English composer, Benjamin Britten.

'The course of true love never did run smooth.' (A Midsummer Night's Dream)

THE CHARACTERS

THE LOVERS

● *HERMIA*

Hermia is a short, dark-haired and happy girl, who is in love with Lysander. However, she has a quick temper and a sharp tongue.

● *LYSANDER & DEMETRIUS*

These young men, in love with both Hermia and Helena at different times in the play, are not very deep characters.

They are full of fighting energy, talk a lot about love, but do little else. Puck's magic plays games with them:

'Up and down, up and down,
I will lead them up and down.
I am feared in field and town.
Goblin, lead them up and down.'

● *HELENA*

Helena is tall, fair-haired and quieter than Hermia. She is desperately in love with Demetrius, who will have nothing to do with her.

● **THESEUS – DUKE OF ATHENS**

> Theseus is the wise and well-loved Duke of Athens. He is sensible, just and kind towards all the people under his rule.

● **HIPPOLYTA – WARRIOR QUEEN**

> Hippolyta is the strong and attractive Queen of the Amazons, a tribe of warrior women in Asia. She is engaged to marry Theseus.

● **THE RUDE MECHANICALS**

> The workmen of Athens are simple, goodhearted, but uneducated men. They decide they will produce a play for their Duke, Theseus, on his wedding day and choose the tragic love story of Pyramus and Thisbe. They practise at night in the wood and then, on the wedding night, the Master of Revels selects their play and they perform it at Court.

Peter **QUINCE**   =   **PROLOGUE**
A Carpenter

Tom **SNOUT**   =   **WALL**
A Tinker

Robin **STARVELING**   =   **MOONSHINE**
A Tailor

SNUG   =   **LION**
A Joiner

46 *'My friends were poor but honest.'* (All's Well That Ends Well)

Nick BOTTOM = PYRAMUS
A Weaver

Bottom is not a very good actor, but he is very enthusiastic and wants to perform all the parts in their play. He overacts at the rehearsal in the wood, and, because he is such an ass, Puck uses his magic to change Bottom's head to look like a donkey's. He is a popular, likeable clown.

Francis FLUTE = THISBE
A Bellows Mender

Flute is a young man who hasn't yet grown a beard and so he has to take the woman's part. This was common in Shakespeare's time, as only men acted on stage. He feels awkward doing this, but the others persuade him to play Thisbe.

After their play before the Duke, the Mechanicals dance a Bergomask, a country dance, which may have been a Maypole or Morris dance like those which are still seen today. The Elizabethans and Jacobeans were very fond of music and dancing and liked to see these in their plays. Shakespeare's plays are full of songs, and actors had to be able to sing and dance well. The plays were often chosen to be performed at Court by the Master of Revels, whose job was to arrange entertainments. Two of the great comic actors of the time, Will Kempe and Richard Tarleton, were famous for their dancing of jigs, which were particularly lively dances. Masques and plays were usually followed by general dancing and merrymaking. Out of the theatre, ordinary people enjoyed these too, whenever there was a holiday.

● THE FAIRIES

'Ill met by moonlight, proud Titania.'

When Shakespeare was alive, most people believed in the supernatural and witchcraft. Fairies were not pretty little floating creatures, but weird spirits who could cast spells on people and cause all sorts of problems. They were thought to be amoral, which meant they did not know the difference between right and wrong. They helped people, or tricked them, just as they chose, and they were said to have strange, cheeky or frightening faces. A hobgoblin, called Puck, is one of the main characters in *A Midsummer Night's Dream*. Shakespeare also calls Puck 'Robin Goodfellow'; this may be because the King and Queen of the May were often called Robin and Marian – after Robin Hood and Maid Marian.

The play's title suggests the action takes place on Midsummer Night, because of the popular belief in 'midsummer madness' and the supernatural things supposed to happen then. But the play actually takes place on May Day, a traditional time of revels throughout Britain and one, like the Midsummer Night of the title, often associated with magic.

OBERON – KING OF THE FAIRIES
All-powerful in the fairy kingdom, Oberon is proud and strong. He uses his magic to help the lovers, but also against the queen, Titania, who has made him jealous and angry.

TITANIA – THE FAIRY QUEEN
Titania is generous, strong and tender, but also stubborn and jealous. She is a beautiful and independent spirit.

PUCK
Puck, the hobgoblin, is Oberon's fairy jester. He is mischievous and loves to play tricks on people for his own amusement.

'Rough winds do shake the darling buds of May' (Sonnet 18)

At the end of the play, when everyone has gone to bed, the fairies go through the palace to bring good luck and bless the marriages. Puck goes first with his broom, to clean up the house.

PUCK:

Now the hungry lion roars,
And the wolf behowls the moon;
Whilst the heavy ploughman snores,
All with weary task fordone.
Now the wasted brands do glow,
Whilst the screech-owl, screeching loud
Puts the wretch that lies in woe
In remembrance of a shroud.
Now it is the time of night
That the graves, all gaping wide,
Every one lets forth its sprite,
In the church-way paths to glide.
And we fairies, that do run
By the triple Hecate's team
From the presence of the sun,
Following darkness like a dream,
Now are frolic. Not a mouse
Shall disturb this hallowed house.
I am sent with broom before,
To sweep the dust behind the door.

'Angels and ministers of grace defend us' (Hamlet)

THE PLOT

The play opens in Athens where Duke Theseus is preparing to marry Hippolyta. Hermia, the daughter of an Athenian citizen called Egeus, is in love with Lysander who loves her. Egeus, however, wants her to marry Demetrius! Demetrius also loves her. There is an ancient law which states that if a daughter will not accept the husband her father chooses for her, she will either be put to death or banished for life to a nunnery (convent). The Duke gives her until his own wedding day to make up her mind what to do.

Lysander and Hermia decide to elope. They will meet in a wood and escape to Lysander's aunt, where they can marry without Egeus's permission. They tell their plan to Helena, Hermia's best friend. Helena, however, is herself in love with Demetrius and tells him of the elopement because she hopes to win his attention and gratitude. Demetrius decides he will go to the wood and stop Lysander and Hermia's marriage: Helena follows him.

Oberon decides to teach Titania a lesson and sends Puck to find the flower Love-in-Idleness, whose juice has magical powers. Oberon drops some of the juice into the eyes of the sleeping Titania. The magic ensures that Titania will fall in love with the first creature she sees when she wakes up and he weaves a spell to make sure she wakes 'when some vile thing is near'.

Demetrius is also in the wood, searching for Hermia; Helena is pestering him. Oberon, overhearing them, feels sorry for Helena and sends Puck to squeeze the magic juice in Demetrius's eyes so he will fall in love with her. Oberon tells Puck he will be able to recognise Demetrius by his Athenian clothes. Unfortunately, Puck sees Lysander, who also wears Athenian clothes, and mistakenly drops the juice in his eyes. When Lysander awakes, the first person he sees is Helena.

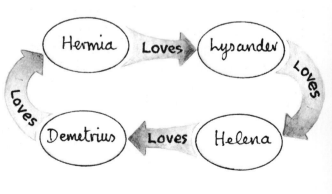

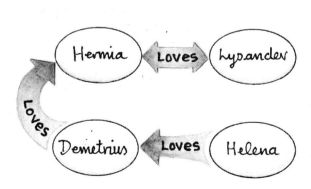

In the wood, Oberon and Titania, King and Queen of the Fairies, have quarrelled.

Puck realises his mistake and tries to correct it by putting some juice into Demetrius's eyes. But Demetrius wakes to see Helena and also falls in love with her. The young men who were in love with Hermia are now

'We that are true lovers run into strange capers.' (As You Like It)

both in love with Helena and the two women are hurt and angry. Each woman thinks that there is a plot to make fun of her.

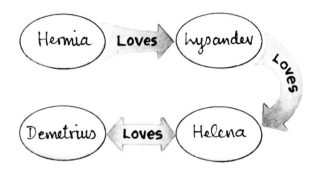

The mischievous Puck has meanwhile been playing jokes elsewhere. In another part of the wood, some Athenian workmen, including Bottom the weaver, have been rehearsing an entertainment, the tale of Pyramus and Thisbe, which they hope to perform for the Duke's wedding. Puck has transformed Bottom's head into that of an ass, because he is such a fool, and Titania has woken up to fall in love with him.

Eventually, thanks to another magic juice, which reverses the spell, everything ends happily. Oberon and Titania make up their quarrel, Puck puts the second juice into Lysander's eyes so that when he wakes up he will again love Hermia, and Bottom's appearance returns to normal. When dawn breaks, the Duke and Hippolyta, who are out hunting, find the lovers who wake as if from a dream.

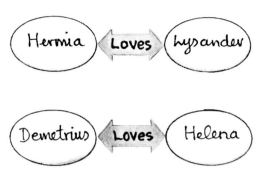

Egeus forgives his daughter, and the lovers are married along with the Duke and Hippolyta. The highlight of the wedding feast is the workmen's play. At midnight, Puck is left alone on stage to speak the last words to the audience. He hopes they have enjoyed the play but, just in case they have not, suggests that perhaps they have been asleep and that everything was just a dream.

PUCK:
> If we shadows have offended
> Think but this, and all is mended!
> That you have but slumbered here,
> While these visions did appear;
> And this weak and idle theme,
> No more yielding but a dream,
> Gentles, do not reprehend.
> If you pardon, we will mend.
> And, as I am an honest Puck,
> If we have unearned luck
> Now to scape the serpent's tongue,
> We will make amends ere long;
> Else the Puck a liar call.
> So, good night unto you all.
> Give me your hands, if we be friends,
> And Robin shall restore amends.

MIDSUMMER NIGHT

People believed that Midsummer Night was an enchanted and magical time when witches and warlocks, ghosts and devils, fairies and evil spirits were out and about. Midsummer Night, the night before 24 June, is an ancient fire-festival celebrated in many parts of Europe. After 21 June, the sun begins to wane. People would often light fires to help the sun stay hot, to drive away evil spirits brought out by the darkness and bring good luck to their farm or business.

Midsummer Day is also the Feast of St John the Baptist, so Midsummer Night is sometimes called St John's Eve. People would celebrate throughout the night. It was considered very lucky to jump through a St John's fire.

In Shakespeare's time, Midsummer Eve was, in fact, 11 days later than it is today. When Julius Caesar organised the calendar in 46 BC, the exact length of a year was not known. Since then, every year had been a few minutes too long. So, in 1752 the English calendar had to jump 11 days in order to catch up. There were widespread riots because the people thought they had lost part of their lives and they demanded 'Give us back our 11 days!' 4 July is now known as Old Midsummer Eve.

'Now is the winter of our discontent . . .' (Richard III)

A COMEDY SCENE
ACT 5, SCENE 1 (abridged)

The tragic story of the lovers, Pyramus and Thisbe

The play within the play

Enter – QUINCE *as the* PROLOGUE
[Flourish of trumpets.]

PROLOGUE: If we offend, it is with our good will.
That you should think, we come not to offend,
But with good will. To show our simple skill,
That is the true beginning of our end.
Consider then, we come but in despite.
We do not come, as minding to content you,
Our true intent is. All for your delight
We are not here. That you should here repent you,
The actors are at hand; and, by their show,
You shall know all, that you are like to know.

Enter – PYRAMUS & THISBE, WALL, MOONSHINE *and LION*
[to mime the story]

PROLOGUE: Gentles, perchance you wonder at this show;
But wonder on, till truth make all things plain.
This man is Pyramus, if you would know;
This beauteous lady Thisbe is, certain.
This man, with lime and rough-cast, doth present
Wall, that vile Wall which did these lovers sunder;
And through Wall's chink, poor souls, they are content
To whisper. At the which let no man wonder.
This man, with lanthorn, dog, and bush of thorn,
Presenteth Moonshine; for, if you will know,
By moonshine did these lovers think no scorn
To meet at Ninus' tomb, there, there to woo.
This grisly beast, which Lion hight by name,
The trusty Thisbe, coming first by night,
Did scare away, or rather did afright;
And as she fled, her mantle she did fall;
Which Lion vile with bloody mouth did stain.
Anon comes Pyramus, sweet youth and tall,
And finds his trusty Thisbe's mantle slain;
Whereat with blade, with bloody blameful blade,
He bravely broached his boiling bloody breast;
And Thisbe, tarrying in mulberry shade,
His dagger drew, and died. For all the rest,
Let Lion, Moonshine, Wall, and lovers twain,
At large discourse while here they do remain.

[Exeunt everyone except WALL*]*

WALL: In this same interlude it doth befall
That I, one Snout by name, present a wall;
And such a wall as I would have you think
That had in it a crannied hole or chink,
Through which the lovers, Pyramus and Thisbe,
Did whisper often very secretly.
This loam, this rough-cast, and this stone, doth show
That I am that same wall; the truth is so;
And this the cranny is, right and sinister,
Through which the fearful lovers are to whisper.

Enter PYRAMUS

PYRAMUS: O grim-looked night! O night with hue so black!
O night, which ever art when day is not!
O night, O night, alack, alack, alack,
I fear my Thisbe's promise is forgot!

And thou, O wall, O sweet, O lovely wall,
That stand'st between her father's ground and mine;
Thou wall, O wall, O sweet and lovely wall,
Show me thy chink, to blink through with mine eyne.
            [WALL *holds up his fingers.*]
Thanks, courteous wall. Jove shield thee well for this
But what see I? No Thisbe do I see.
O wicked wall, through whom I see no bliss;
Cursed be thy stones for thus deceiving me!

Enter THISBE

THISBE: O wall, full often hast thou heard my moans,
             For parting my fair Pyramus and me!
             My cherry lips have often kissed thy stones,
             Thy stones with lime and hair knit up in thee.

PYRAMUS: I see a voice; now will I to the chink,
             To spy an I can hear my Thisbe's face.
             Thisbe!

THISBE: My love! thou art my love, I think.

PYRAMUS: Think what thou wilt, I am thy lover's grace;
             And like Limander am I trusty still.

THISBE: And I like Helen, till the Fates me kill.

PYRAMUS: O kiss me through the hole of this vile wall.

THISBE: I kiss the wall's hole, not your lips at all.

PYRAMUS: Wilt thou at Ninny's tomb meet me straightway?

THISBE: 'Tide life, 'tide death, I come without delay.

WALL: Thus have I, Wall, my part discharged so;
             And, being done, thus Wall away doth go.

Exit WALL   *Enter* LION & MOONSHINE

LION: You, ladies, you, whose gentle hearts do fear
             The smallest monstrous mouse that creeps on floor,
             May now, perchance, both quake and tremble here,
             When Lion rough in wildest rage doth roar.
             Then know that I, one Snug the joiner, am
             A lion fell, nor else no lion's dam;
             For, if I should as lion come in strife
             Into this place, 'twere pity on my life.

MOONSHINE: This lanthorn doth the hornéd moon present –

DEMETRIUS: He should have worn the horns on his head!

MOONSHINE: This lanthorn doth the hornéd moon present;
              Myself the Man in the Moon do seem to be.

THESEUS: The man should be put into the lantern.
              How is it else the man in the moon?

HIPPOLYTA: I am a-weary of this moon. Would he would change!

MOONSHINE: All that I have to say, is, to tell you that the lanthorn is
              the moon; I, the Man in the Moon; this thorn-bush,
              my thorn-bush; and this dog, my dog.

Enter THISBE

THISBE: This is old Ninny's tomb. Where is my love?

Enter LION – *roaring.*   THISBE *runs off.*
LION *tears* THISBE'*s mantle and then exits.*

Enter PYRAMUS

PYRAMUS: Sweet Moon, I thank thee for thy sunny beams;
              I thank thee, Moon, for shining now so bright;
              For, by thy gracious, golden, glittering gleams,
              I trust to take of truest Thisbe sight.
                       But stay, O spite!
                       But mark, poor knight,
              What dreadful dole is here!
                       Eyes, do you see?
                       How can it be?
              O dainty duck! O dear!
                       Thy mantle good,
                       What! stained with blood?
              Approach, ye Furies fell.
                       O Fates! come, come;
                       Cut thread and thrum;
              Quail, crush, conclude, and quell.
              O wherefore, Nature, didst thou lions frame?
              Since lion vile hath here deflowered my dear;
              Which is – no, no – which was the fairest dame
              That lived, that loved, that liked, that looked with cheer

Come, tears, confound;
    Out, sword, and wound
    The pap of Pyramus;
    Ay, that left pap,
    Where heart doth hop.   [*Stabs himself*]
Thus die I, thus, thus, thus.
    Now am I dead,
    Now am I fled;
My soul is in the sky.
    Tongue, lose thy light;
    Moon, take thy flight.   [*Exit* MOONSHINE]
Now die, die, die, die, die. [*Dies*]

Enter THISBE

THISBE:
    Asleep, my love?
    What, dead, my dove?
O Pyramus, arise,
    Speak, speak. Quite dumb?
    Dead, dead? A tomb
Must cover thy sweet eyes.
    These lily lips,
    This cherry nose,
These yellow cowslip cheeks,
    Are gone, are gone;
    Lovers, make moan;
His eyes were green as leeks.
    O Sisters Three,
    Come, come to me,
With hands as pale as milk;
    Lay them in gore,
    Since you have shore
With shears his thread of silk.
    Tongue, not a word.
    Come, trusty sword;
Come, blade, my breast imbrue.   [*Stabs herself*]
    And farewell, friends;
    Thus Thisbe ends;
Adieu, adieu, adieu. [*Dies*]

Masks and make-up in theatre history

Modern theatre dates back to the religious processions and ceremonies of the Ancient Greeks. Their plays were performed out of doors in the Greek countryside with huge audiences seated on the slopes of the surrounding hills. Because the spectators were so far away, the actors had to appear larger than life. They wore enormous high-soled boots, tall headdresses, wigs and masks. The masks told the audience which type of character was being played – male or female, young or old, happy or sad, and so on.

The Romans continued the Greek traditions of theatre but with some very important alterations. In Greek times, deaths always occurred *offstage*: the 'corpse' was wheeled on afterwards. But the Romans liked to see the killing happening before their eyes. Of course, the victims were not played by actors but by criminals and slaves who were actually killed during the play.

After the Romans, there is little or no record of any theatre until the late thirteenth century when the Church began to encourage new forms of drama. Plays known as Miracle or Mystery plays became popular, based on stories from the Bible or on legends of the saints. By the fifteenth century, the Miracles had been joined by the Moralities, where characters represented human vices or virtues.

Other forms of theatre also developed. Short dramatic Interludes, which took place during the intervals of religious plays, now became popular in their own right and were taken round by groups of strolling players. There were Mummers' plays and, by the reign of Elizabeth I, there were entertainments involving dancing and disguises which were called Masques. The actors in these Masques were amateurs and performed them using very elaborate masks: Masques were very popular at Court. In some of Shakespeare's plays, characters disguise themselves with masks – for example, Romeo goes masked to the Capulet ball where he meets Juliet.

A masque at Sir Henry Upton's wedding, in Shakespeare's time.

'To dance attendance on their lordships' pleasures.' (Henry VIII)

By Shakespeare's time, actors were using a certain amount of stage make-up. The actor playing Othello, for example, would darken his skin with soot; peasants would be stained with a brown earth pigment called 'umber'; ghosts would have chalk on their faces, while the noses of drunks would be reddened with powder. And it is likely that boys playing women would also have rouged cheeks and lips. But, most of the time, wigs, beards, costumes and props were used to show who the characters were. In *A Midsummer Night's Dream*, Bottom tries to decide which beard would best suit his portrayal of Pyramus, ' . . . either your straw-colour beard, your orange-tawny beard, your purple-in-grain beard, or your French-crown-colour beard, your perfect yellow.'

Many people thought make-up was an insult to God. It is possible that Shakespeare himself may not have cared very much for the Elizabethan fashion of painting the face. Hermia, in *A Midsummer Night's Dream*, insults Helena, referring to her make-up by calling her, 'thou painted maypole'.

When performances moved indoors, in the seventeenth century, artificial lighting (candles and oil) made make-up all the more necessary so that audiences could see the actors' faces clearly. But until Ludwig Leichner invented **greasepaint** in 1865, and theatres began to be lit by the nineteenth century invention of gas-lights, make-up continued to be powder mixed with grease, or harmful white lead.

Today, most actors will, at some time, have used the sticks, tins or tubes of Leichner make-up, each with its own shade or colour. However, with the vast improvements in theatre lighting, many actors now rely upon non-greasy **cake** make-up and ordinary eyebrow pencils bought from the local chemist.

COSTUMES FOR
A MIDSUMMER NIGHT'S DREAM

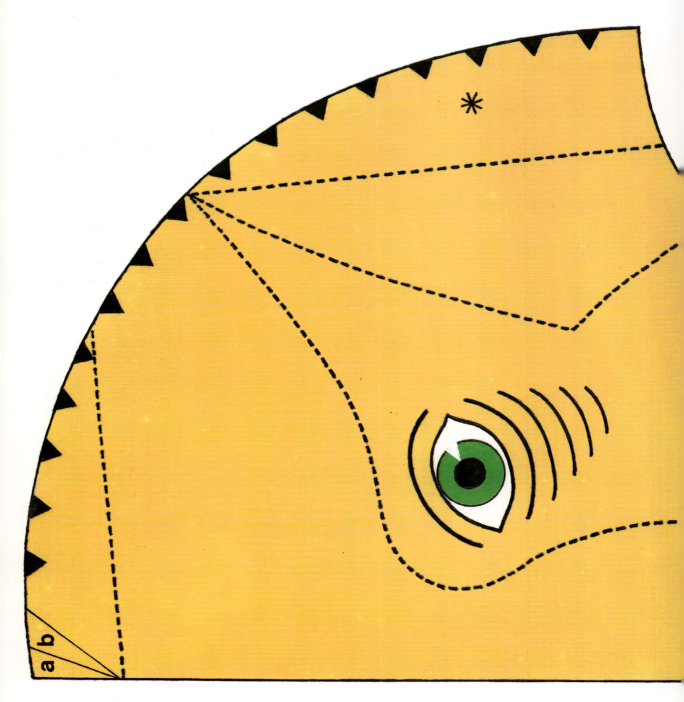

'A harmless, necessary cat.' (The Merchant of Venice)

● *LION'S MASK*

Trace the outline below.
Fold a sheet of thin card.
Transfer the outline to one side of the card, making sure the fold is against the nose side of the mask. Cut round outline, taking care not to cut along the fold.

Open out whole mask and transfer details to the other side.

Score all dotted lines lightly, then fold backwards.

Stick down (a) face to face with (b).

Take a strip of thick card and make a head band.

Attach the mask to the head band with staples at the points marked *. Make sure that the points of the staples are on the outside.

Attach elastic at the points marked *, to go under the chin.

The mask should be worn on the forehead so the wearer's face can be seen. The mane covers the back of the head and shoulders.

Cut some pipe cleaners in half and attach to each side as whiskers, if required.

Roll nose under, round index finger.

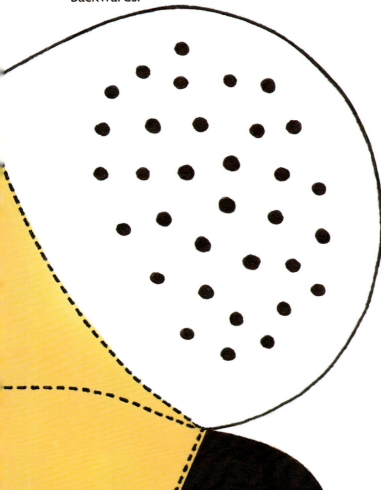

● LION'S MANE

1 Cut out this shape from any material.

Attach mane to the edge of the Lion's mask where there are darts (▼) by using a stapler, glue, or sticky tape. Turn the edge of the mane under as you do this. Make sure the points of the staples are on the outside.

Store the whole mask on a skittle or upturned stool while painting and sticking.

2 Cut a number of strips out of paper.

Curl the paper round a pencil or finger. You can also do this by holding one end of each strip and running a ruler or scissors along it.

3 Attach the curls with glue to the material. *Start at the bottom* and work upwards.

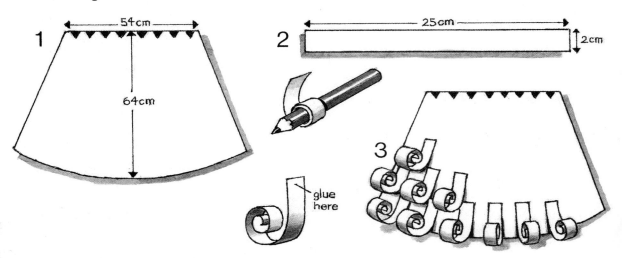

● LION'S SUIT

The lion can wear ordinary Elizabethan costume (see p. 85). However, an adult's old brown coat can easily be made into an animal's costume.

Cut a slit partway up the centre of the back (from the bottom). Sew fronts and backs together to make legs. Sew under crutch area. Join rest of front together with Velcro, buttons, zip or even safety pins.

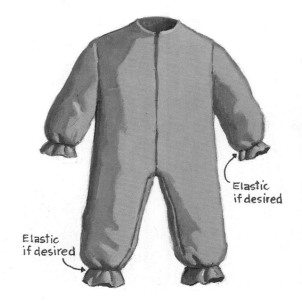

'The cat will mew and dog will have his day.' (Hamlet)

● *MOONSHINE COSTUME ACCESSORIES*

The lantern and thorn bush are attached to the broom handle. The toy dog is trailed by the lead.

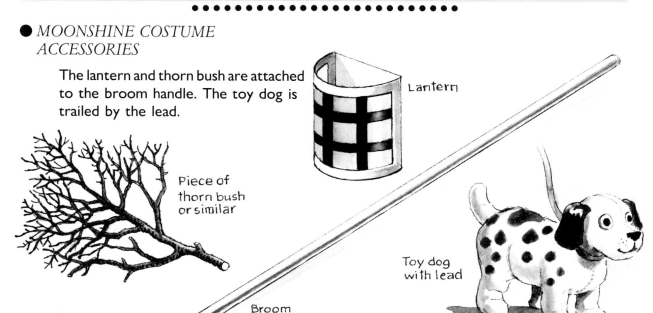

Lantern

Piece of thorn bush or similar

Toy dog with lead

Broom handle

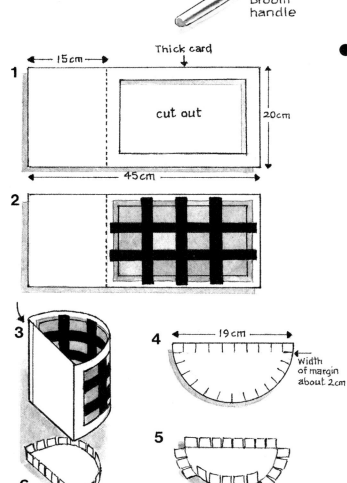

Thick card

1 ← 15cm → 45cm 20cm cut out

2

3

4 ← 19cm → Width of margin about 2cm

5

6

● *LANTERNS*

These can easily be made as follows.

1 Take a piece of thick card. Score and cut as shown on the left.

2 Stick sheet of tracing paper over 'window'.

Turn over. Stick black insulating tape on other side.

3 Stick two ends of card together using masking tape (or Sellotape) inside.

Bottom of lantern:

4 Cut a semi-circle of card to size shown.

5 Cut along each little line as shown. Bend each section upwards.

6 Fit teeth inside bottom and stick in place with tape.

'A snapper-up of unconsidered trifles.' (The Winter's Tale)

● *PUCK'S COSTUME*

This costume is simple and effective.

1 Trace this leaf onto thin card and cut it out to make a template.

Draw round it on different shades of green and brown paper. Cut out the leaves.

2 Cut the feet off a pair of thick tights (green or brown). Stick the leaves on, starting from the bottom of the legs and working upwards: Copydex is the best glue for this. Overlap the leaves.

It is easiest to stick the leaves on while someone is actually wearing the tights.

This costume is quite tough and is worn with nothing above (if a boy) or with a top covered with leaves in the same way (for girls). The leaves can, of course, be made from material.

Start here

● WALL COSTUME

EITHER A

Cut base costume from an old cotton sheet. Draw outline of bricks directly on, using a template. Paint bricks in different shades of quite thick powder paint.

OR B

Make a template for bricks. Draw round this on different coloured material. Cut out bricks and stick onto base costume with glue. Arrange bricks as shown.

OPTIONAL EXTRA

For the head – worn with elastic under chin. A circle of card rests just below the rim of a plastic flowerpot. The flower goes through a hole in the centre of the card and into a lump of Plasticine at the base of the pot.

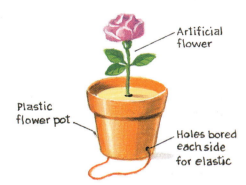

Distance between shoulder and knee

cut head hole

Length from one hand to other across shoulders with arms outstretched

Artificial flower

Plastic flower pot

Holes bored each side for elastic

● MOB CAP AND PLAITS FOR THISBE

Cut a circle at least twice the circumference of the head, from an old piece of material. With thin elastic, sew a running stitch round the outside edge leaving a border of about 5cm, and gather up to fit over the head. Using wool, raffia or crepe paper rolls, make two plaits. Attach one end of each plait to the underside of the mob cap, and tie ribbons to the other ends.

● A ROMAN HELMET FOR PYRAMUS

Make a card head band that fits snugly. Using strips of thin card, and sticking them with masking tape, build up the shape of the helmet. For the crest, fold tissue or crepe paper into four and cut along one edge making a fringe. This is stuck to the top. Paint the helmet in silver paint.

More ideas on costume-making can be found on pages 84-87.

'Uneasy lies the head that wears the crown . . .' (Henry IV, Part 2)

MAKING MUSIC

● *YOU SPOTTED SNAKES WITH DOUBLE TONGUE*

This is a simple modern setting, with chords for guitar or tuned percussion, of the fairies' lullaby for Titania in Act 2, Scene 2. It can be played on recorders, or sung, in two parts, with glockenspiel and percussion accompaniment; or it can simply be sung in unison to an accompaniment of Indian bells, triangles, or any light-sounding percussion. Home-made instruments such as half-full glasses or milk bottles tapped with spoons, and dried peas, rice or lentils rolled back-and forwards or shaken inside empty plastic detergent bottles or yoghurt pots, can often do just as well. It is worth looking around to see what sounds can be achieved from everyday objects.

YOU SPOTTED SNAKES WITH DOUBLE TONGUE

You spotted snakes with double tongue,
Thorny hedgehogs, be not seen;
Newts and blind worms, do no wrong,
Come not near our fairy Queen.

Chorus
Philomel with melody
Sing in our sweet lullaby.
Lulla, lulla, lullaby;
Lulla, lulla, lullaby.
Never harm nor spell nor charm
Come our lovely lady nigh.
So good night, with lullaby.

Weaving spiders, come not here;
Hence, you long-legg'd spinners, hence.
Beetles black, approach not near;
Worm nor snail do no offence.
(Chorus)

'If music be the food of love, play on.' (Twelfth Night)

TWO PART VERSION FOR DESCANT RECORDERS OR VOICES

Macbeth

● ● ● ● ● ●

THE SOURCE OF THE PLAY

Shakespeare's play seems to have been largely inspired by *The Chronicles of England, Scotland and Ireland*, published in 1577 by the sixteenth-century historian, Raphael Holinshed. These chronicles were a mixture of fact and legend but Shakespeare was not too worried about historical truth. Not only did he take elements of different stories, but he also used Holinshed's own words when it suited him.

MACBETH

Shakespeare's *Macbeth* has been the inspiration for at least three operas. The most famous of these is by Guiseppe Verdi and was first produced in Florence in 1847. *Symphonic poem*, by the composer Richard Strauss, is also based on the play.

'Double, double, toil and trouble;
Fire burn and cauldron bubble.' (Macbeth)

The real Macbeth

The main characters of the play did exist. King Duncan I of Scotland died in 1040, probably killed by Macbeth. However, there is some considerable doubt about Banquo's existence. He was probably invented by an early fifteenth-century historian. Holinshed names Banquo as a Stuart ancestor. Shakespeare was happy to continue the idea and make him a very noble character in order to please his new patron, King James I of England and VI of Scotland. The real Macbeth was a good, strong king and not the evil character of Shakespeare's play.

The idea of the wood that moves (Birnam Wood in the play) is found in much older stories and was well known in folk tales. The Three Witches would also have been readily accepted by Elizabethan audiences who firmly believed in witchcraft.

It is interesting to compare the scene in Shakespeare's play, when Macbeth and Banquo first meet the Three Witches, with the following extract from Holinshed's *Chronicles*.

Shortlie after happened a strange and vncouth woonder, which afterward was the cause of much trouble in the realme of Scotland, as ye shall after heare. It fortuned as Makbeth and Banquho iournied towards Fores, where the king then laie, they went sporting by the waie togither without other companie, saue onelie themselues, passing thorough the woods and fields, when suddenlie in the middest of a laund, there met them three women in strange and wild apparell, resembling creatures of elder world, whome when they attentiuelie beheld, woondering much at the sight, the first of them spake and said: *"All haile, Makbeth, thane of Glammis!"* (for he had latelie entered into that dignitie and office by the death of his father Sinell). The second of them said: *"Haile, Makbeth, thane of Cawder!"* But the third said: *"All haile, Makbeth, that heereafter shalt be king of Scotland!"*

THE CHARACTERS

● *MACBETH*

Macbeth's character changes throughout the play. At first we see him as a brave soldier – noble and loyal to King Duncan. Unfortunately, he is also weak and easily influenced by others. The Witches' prophecies suggest that he can himself become king. Spurred on by Lady Macbeth, he murders King Duncan and sinks deeper and deeper into evil. However, he meets his death bravely in a fight with Macduff, whose family he has had murdered.

● *LADY MACBETH*

Lady Macbeth also changes character during the play. At first, she is a scheming, ambitious woman, cool and calm before the murder of Duncan. However, his death and the terrible killings which follow drive her out of her mind. She has nightmares and she sleepwalks. In the end, she cannot bear to live with the knowledge of what she and her husband have done and she kills herself.

● *BANQUO*

Like his friend Macbeth, Banquo is a brave and noble soldier. When they meet the Witches, he is told his children will be kings. Unlike Macbeth, however, he does not turn to evil. Banquo is also slow to see evil in others and does not suspect Macbeth of the King's murder until it is too late. Macbeth hires men to murder Banquo and his son, Fleance, in order to stop his part of the prophecies coming true. Fleance, however, escapes.

● *MACDUFF*

Macduff is another noble lord, an honest and brave man, who suspects more quickly than Banquo that it is Macbeth who has murdered the King. He joins Duncan's son, Malcolm, in England, leaving his wife and children at home. Macbeth has them murdered and Macduff returns, determined on revenge. He turns out to be the man whom the Witches describe as 'not of woman born', destined to kill Macbeth at the end of the play.

● *KING DUNCAN*

Duncan is a good king, loyal and generous to his friends, and a just and honest man. In contrast to Macbeth, he does nothing to deserve his violent death.

● *THE THREE WITCHES*

The Witches, also known as the Weird Sisters, are mysterious creatures whom Macbeth and Banquo meet on their return from battle at the beginning of the play. They might be real or they might be evil spirits. They speak the prophecies which plant ideas in Macbeth's mind and lead him to commit murder.

THE PLOT

As Macbeth and his fellow nobleman, Banquo, return from battle, they come across the Three Witches. These strange creatures greet Macbeth first by the title he already has – Thane of Glamis – and then by the title of another nobleman – Thane of Cawdor. Finally, they suggest to the astonished Macbeth that he will 'be King hereafter'. To Banquo they offer the startling news that, although he will never be king himself, his descendants will rule Scotland.

The Witches vanish into the mist, and Macbeth is brought the news that the Thane of Cawdor has been killed and that he has been given the title. The Witches' first prophecy has now come true. Macbeth wonders about the possibility of the second.

Macbeth sends a letter home to his wife telling her what the Witches have said. Lady Macbeth also learns that King Duncan is to pay them a visit. She realises that this could be the perfect opportunity to murder Duncan and have her husband crowned king.

Lady Macbeth is more determined than her husband and persuades him to carry out the murder. Despite several changes of mind, Macbeth at last agrees and, while the King sleeps, stabs him to death. Macbeth is appalled at what he has done and loses his nerve. Lady Macbeth takes his dagger and smears the sleeping guards with the King's blood.

Not long afterwards, the King's butchered body is discovered by Macduff. Macbeth, apparently overcome with grief, kills the guards. Duncan's sons, Malcolm and Donalbain, fear for their own lives and flee: Malcolm goes to England and Donalbain to Ireland, leaving Macbeth to be crowned king.

Although at first the guards had been thought to be responsible for Duncan's death, suspicion gradually begins to fall on Macbeth. It is Banquo who eventually becomes the most suspicious.

Macbeth remembers the Witches' prophecy about Banquo and decides that he also must die. At a banquet at the castle, Macbeth learns that his men have murdered Banquo, but that Banquo's son, Fleance, has escaped. Macbeth is horrified when Banquo's ghost, invisible to everyone else, takes his place at the banqueting table. Macbeth is very disturbed and visibly shaken, so much so that his courtiers think that he is ill.

Deeply frightened, Macbeth returns to the Witches. They show him ghostly apparitions which warn him against Macduff who has now joined forces with Malcolm in England. They also tell him that 'no man of woman born, Shall harm Macbeth'. From the third apparition, he learns that he can never be defeated until 'Great Birnam Wood to high Dunsinane Hill, Shall come against him'. Knowing that trees cannot move themselves, Macbeth feels safe. However, the final apparition shows Banquo with a row of kings and once more Macbeth recalls the Witches' prophecy.

This time Macbeth cannot turn to his wife for help. Her conscience is troubling her and she is gradually going mad. Macbeth decides to have Lady Macduff and her children murdered. In England, Macduff vows vengeance.

Macbeth still believes that nobody can defeat him. He does not know that English soldiers are already in Birnam Wood preparing to attack him. They cut down branches to use as camouflage and, as they approach the castle, the woods appear to move.

Lady Macbeth, whose mind has now completely gone, commits suicide. The castle surrenders to the army, but Macbeth fights on. He comes face to face with Macduff and tells him that his life is safe against anyone 'of woman born'. Macduff's chilling answer is

that he did not have a normal birth but was taken prematurely from his mother's womb.

Macbeth now realises that he must fight for his life. He draws his sword, but in vain. Macduff kills him, cuts off his head and takes it to Malcolm as proof that Macbeth is dead. As the play ends, Malcolm is hailed King of Scotland.

On the morow when Makbeth beheld them comming in this sort, hee first marueyled what the matter ment, but in the end remembred himselfe, that the prophecie which he had hearde long before that time, of the comming of Byrnane wood to Dunsinnane Castell, was likely to bee now fulfilled. Neuerthelesse, he brought hys men in order of battell, and exhorted them to doe valiantly, howbeit his enimies had scarcely cast from them their boughes, when Makbeth percei-uing their numbers betook him streight to flight, whom Makduffe pursued with great hatred euē till he came vnto Lunfannain, where Makbeth perceiuing that Makduffe was hard at his back, leapt beside his horse. saying, thou traytor, what meaneth it that thou shouldest thus in vaine fol-low me that am not appoynted to be slain by a-ny creature that is borne of a woman, come on therefore, and receyue thy rewarde which thou hast deserued for thy paynes, and therewithall he lyfted vp his swoorde thinking to haue slaine him. But Makduffe quickly auoyding from his horse, ere he came at him, answered (with his na-ked swoorde in his hande) saying : it is true Mak-beth, and now shall thine insatiable crueltie haue an end, for I am euen he that thy wysardes haue tolde thee of, who was neuer borne of my mo-ther, but ripped out of her woombe : therewithall he stept vnto him, & slue him in the place. Then cutting his heade from the shoulders, hee set it vpon a poll, and brought it vnto Malcolme. This was the end of Makbeth, after he had raig-ned .xvij. yeares ouer the Scottishmen.

Makbeth set-teth his men in order of battell. Makbeth flee-eth, and is pur-sued of Mak-duffe.

Makbeth is slaine.

MACDUFF:/Turn, hell-hound, turn.
MACBETH:/ Of all men else I have avoided thee.
But get thee back; my soul is too much charg'd
With blood of thine already.
MACDUFF:/I have no words –
My voice is my sword: thou bloodier villain
Than terms can give thee out.

[Fight. Alarum.]

MACBETH:/Thou losest labour.
As easy mayst thou the intrenchant air
With thy keen sword impress as make me bleed.
Let fall thy blade on vulnerable crests;
I bear a charmed life, which must not yield
To one of woman born.
MACDUFF:/Despair thy charm;
And let the angel whom thou still hast serv'd
Tell thee Macduff was from his mother's womb
Untimely ripp'd.
MACBETH:/Accursed be that tongue that tells me so,
For it hath cow'd my better part of man;
And be these juggling fiends no more believ'd
That palter with us in a double sense,
That keep the word of promise to our ear,
And break it to our hope! I'll not fight with thee.
MACDUFF:/Then yield thee, coward,
And live to be the show and gaze o' th' time.
We'll have thee, as our rarer monsters are,
Painted upon a pole, and underwrit
'Here may you see the tyrant'.
MACBETH:/I will not yield,
To kiss the ground before young Malcolm's feet
And to be baited with the rabble's curse.
Though Birnam wood be come to Dunsinane,
And thou oppos'd, being of no woman born,
Yet I will try the last. Before my body
I throw my warlike shield. Lay on, Macduff;
And damn'd be him that first cries 'Hold, enough!'

[Exeunt, fighting. Alarums.]

This is the account of Macbeth's death as it appeared in the first edition of Holinshed's Chronicles *(left), and (right) in the final scene of Shakespeare's* Macbeth.

PART OF THE WITCHES' SCENE FROM ACT 1, SCENE 3

SCENE: *A blasted heath in Scotland. Thunder.*
Enter MACBETH *and* BANQUO.

MACBETH: So foul and fair a day I have not seen.

BANQUO: How far is't called to Forres? What are these,
So wither'd, and so wild in their attire,
That look not like the inhabitants of the earth,
And yet are on't? Live you, or are you aught
That man may question? You seem to understand me,
By each at once her choppy finger laying
Upon her skinny lips. You should be women,
And yet your beards forbid me to interpret
That you are so.

MACBETH: Speak, if you can. What are you?

1st WITCH: All hail, Macbeth! Hail to thee, Thane of Glamis!

2nd WITCH: All hail, Macbeth! Hail to thee, Thane of Cawdor!

3rd WITCH: All hail, Macbeth, that shalt be King hereafter!

BANQUO: Good sir, why do you start, and seem to fear
Things that do sound so fair? In the name of truth,
Are ye fantastical, or that indeed
Which outwardly ye show? My noble partner
You greet with present grace and great prediction
Of noble having and of royal hope,
That he seems rapt withal. To me you speak not.

If you can look into the seeds of time
And say which grain will grow and which will not,
Speak then to me, who neither beg nor fear
Your favours nor your hate.

1st WITCH: Hail!

2nd WITCH: Hail!

3rd WITCH: Hail!

1st WITCH: Lesser than Macbeth, and greater.

2nd WITCH: Not so happy, yet much happier.

3rd WITCH: Thou shalt get kings, though thou be none.
              So, all hail, Macbeth and Banquo!

1st WITCH: Banquo and Macbeth, all hail!

MACBETH: Stay, you imperfect speakers, tell me more.
              By Sinel's death I know I am Thane of Glamis;
              But how of Cawdor? The Thane of Cawdor lives,
              A prosperous gentleman; and to be King
              Stands not within the prospect of belief,
              No more than to be Cawdor. Say from whence
              You owe this strange intelligence, or why
              Upon this blasted heath you stop our way
              With such prophetic greeting? Speak, I charge you.

                        [*The* WITCHES *vanish*]

BANQUO: The earth hath bubbles, as the water has,
              And these are of them. Whither are they vanish'd?

MACBETH: Into the air; and what seemed corporal melted
              As breath into the wind. Would they had stayed!

BANQUO: Were such things here as we do speak about?
              Or have we eaten on the insane root
              That takes the reason prisoner?

MACBETH: Your children shall be kings.

BANQUO: You shall be King.

MACBETH: And Thane of Cawdor too; went it not so?

THEATRICAL SUPERSTITIONS

People who work in theatres are well known for being superstitious. They believe in not tempting fate in case things go wrong during a performance. It is natural to feel nervous of making a mistake in front of a lot of people.

Some superstitions are obviously based on practical common sense. Others do not seem to have any sensible reason behind them. For example, a way of avoiding bad luck when a mistake has been made is to leave the room and close the door. You then knock on the door and must not re-enter until asked.

It is unlucky . . .

. . . to have real flowers on stage

It is also not very sensible. Real flowers would soon wilt and die under the heat from the stage lighting.

. . . to use real mirrors on stage

Again, this is common sense. Real mirrors would reflect the stage lights and cause all sorts of problems. Actually, real mirrors *are* sometimes used but only after they have been rubbed over with soap to make them cloudy. And what if one broke? Apart from the seven years' bad luck, a superstition we all know, imagine the problems of clearing all the glass from the stage where actors might be going barefoot or lying down on the boards.

. . . to wish anyone 'good luck'

If you wish actors good luck they tend to believe that just the opposite will happen so they are quite likely to wish colleagues bad luck as they go on stage. For example, they often say 'Break a leg!'

. . . to whistle in a theatre

Again, there is quite a sensible reason for this. The sound of whistling is piercing and can carry a long way. In some theatres, whistling in the dressing room might be heard not just on stage but also in the audience.

. . . to say the word 'Macbeth'

Except in the lines of the play itself, actors will not say the word 'Macbeth'. They always refer to the play as 'The Scottish Play' instead. There are many stories of productions of this play where terrible things went wrong. The legends have been handed down and it is now widely believed that even to mention the play can bring bad luck!

. . . to quote from *Macbeth*

Actors who go round saying 'Double, double, toil and trouble', and 'What bloody man is that?' (or other famous lines from the play) can be unpopular. There is a story that one of England's greatest actors, Sir Laurence Olivier, used to delight in greeting everyone when he entered a theatre with quotations from *Macbeth*. It is unlikely, though, that anyone would have dared to tell him not to do this. It is also unlikely that anyone knows for certain where these superstitions began.

Producing
a play

● ● ● ● ● ●

'Suit the action to the word, the word to the action.' (Hamlet)

In the theatre
● ● ● ● ● ●

Proscenium arch

Gallery

Circle

Dress circle

Pass door

Stage

Apron stage

Orchestra pit

Stalls

FRONT OF HOUSE

The auditorium. Where the audience sits. 'Out front' means in the audience.

GALLERY OR THE GODS

The highest circle of seats and also the cheapest.

CIRCLE

The next circle of seats above the dress circle.

DRESS CIRCLE

The lowest circle of seats 'upstairs' and often the most expensive. It is called the dress circle because people who sat there used to wear evening dress.

STALLS

The 'downstairs' seats on the ground floor.

PROSCENIUM ARCH ('Pros')

The rectangular 'window' onto the stage. The audience looks through this at the action on the stage.

STAGE

The platform where the performance takes place.

APRON STAGE

Extra bit of the stage sticking out into the audience.

ORCHESTRA PIT

A deep ditch between audience and stage, where the musicians sit.

PASS DOOR

A door which leads from the auditorium to the side of the stage. Usually marked 'Private' or 'No Entry'.

BOX OFFICE

Where the audience buys the tickets.

STAGE DOOR

A door at the back or side of the theatre where the actors enter to go to their dressing rooms.

BACKSTAGE

The part of the theatre behind the stage which the audience does not see. This is where the dressing rooms are and where the scenery is stored.

THEATRE-IN-THE-ROUND

A stage with the audience sitting all round it.

Behind the scenes

• • • • • •

ACTORS' NAMES FOR PARTS OF THE STAGE

Actors write the abbreviations on their scripts so that they know where to enter, exit, stand or move on stage (e.g. Exit SL).

	Back wall			Upstage US ↑
	USR Upstage right	**USC** Upstage centre	**USL** Upstage Left	
Wings	**SR** Stage right	**CS** Centre stage	**SL** Stage left	Wings
Opposite prompt side O P	**DSR** Downstage right	**DSC** Downstage centre	**DSL** Downstage left	Prompt side
	Front of stage			**DS** Downstage ↓
	Audience			

• • • • • •

LIGHTING

SPOTLIGHTS ('SPOTS')
Lights with narrow beams that can light up a particular place or actor.

FLOODS
Rows of lights in metal boxes hanging above the stage for lighting a large area.

LIMELIGHTS or LIMES
Spotlights that can move and follow an actor round the stage. The name comes from the fact that these lights originally used quicklime. Today they are usually called 'follow spots'.

FOOTLIGHTS or FLOATS
Rows of 'floods' along the floor at the front of the stage.

'But, soft! What light through yonder window breaks!' (Romeo and Juliet)

① THE DIRECTOR

Someone who decides where actors shall move on the stage and how they shall play their parts. The director is the person who determines exactly how the play shall be staged.

② THE PRODUCER

Someone who arranges for a play to be put on.

③ STAGE MANAGER (SM)

Once the play opens, the stage manager is in charge of the actual performances (The Run), and looks after everything on or around the stage.

④ ASSISTANT STAGE MANAGER (ASM)

The Assistant Stage Manager is the general dogsbody! He or she does all the fetching and carrying (makes the tea, rattles the thunder sheet, takes messages, calls actors, takes phone messages, sometimes prompts and so on).

⑤ WARDROBE MISTRESS

Someone who cares for and repairs the costumes.

⑥ DRESSER

Someone who helps an actor to put on, or change, costumes.

⑦ LIGHTING OPERATOR

Someone who works the lights – either from the side of the stage or from a box behind the audience.

SET DESIGNER (not illustrated)

The person responsible for designing the scenery and stage sets.

⑧ STAGE HANDS

These are people who put the scenery together before the performances of the play begin and take it down after the last performance. They also help to move scenery, if necessary, during a performance.

'We cannot all be masters.' (Othello)

Making costumes

● ● ● ● ● ●

These basic Elizabethan costumes are cheap and easy to make. Not all productions of Shakespeare's plays need Elizabethan costume – many are set in other periods, and in some performances nowadays modern dress is used. The ideas here can be a useful starting point for designing costumes. (There are suggestions for suitable materials on page 87.)

● ● ● ● ● ●

MAN'S COSTUME

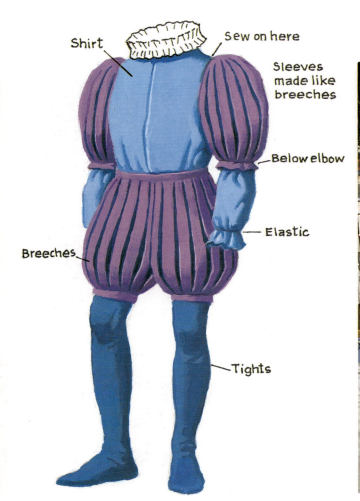

Shirt
Sew on here
Sleeves made like breeches
Below elbow
Elastic
Breeches
Tights

'For the apparel oft proclaims the man' (Hamlet)

ELIZABETHAN BREECHES

These are best made out of thick material such as felt.

Cut rectangle of material.
Width – overlapping round waist.
Length – waist to just below knee.

1 Fold top edge and sew. Leave enough space for threading elastic later.

2 Cut up a centre line from bottom edge until top hem is reached.

3 Fold and sew bottom two edges, as above. This can be done by hand or machine.

4 Draw lines (felt tip best) the width of a metre stick from top to bottom hems.

5 Cut along these lines. DO NOT cut the hems!

6 Cut three pieces of elastic (one for waist, two for thighs)

7 Attach one end of elastic (A) to material with a safety pin.

8 Attach the other end (B) to another safety pin.

9 Thread elastic through waist and thigh hems. The pin makes this easier.

10 Tie both ends (A and B) together.

Wear breeches over coloured tights.

Breeches are simple: young people can easily make them.

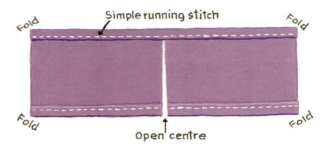

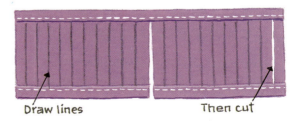

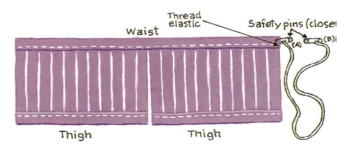

WOMAN'S COSTUME

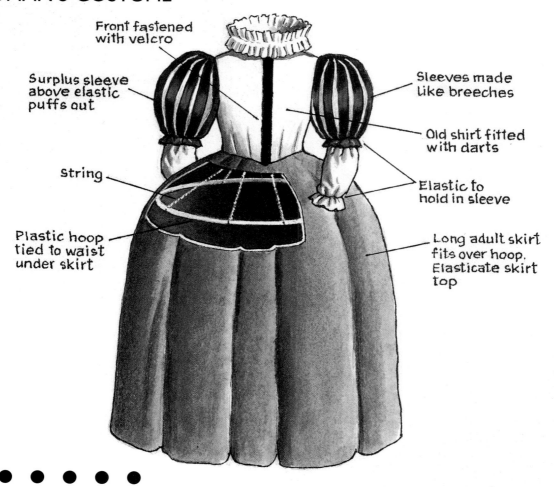

Front fastened with velcro

Surplus sleeve above elastic puffs out

string

Plastic hoop tied to waist under skirt

Sleeves made like breeches

Old shirt fitted with darts

Elastic to hold in sleeve

Long adult skirt fits over hoop. Elasticate skirt top

RUFFS

Use a long strip of white sheet.

Sew two lines of thin elastic in a running stitch along the centre of the strip. Pull to gather the material so that it ruffles up. Fasten the ends of the elastic.

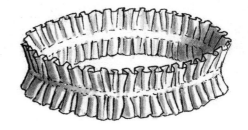

Sew

THIN ELASTIC THREAD

Pull to gather then fasten

Sew

SEWING DARTS

Sew dotted lines together. Taper to a point each end. Do this back and front. *Sew always on the inside.* The darts pull the shirt into the body shape. You can pin the dotted lines together first and check that the shirt fits before sewing. Then you can alter the dart before it is too late.

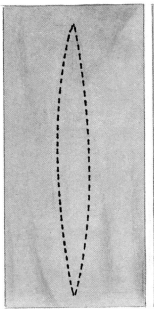 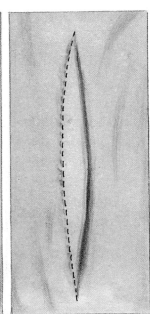

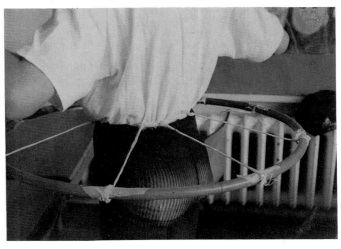

The simplest way to make a woman's skirt stand away from the hips is to tie a hoop around the waist.

OLD SHEETS are good for making costumes.

JUMBLE SALES are a rich source of potential costumes.

MEN'S SHIRTS are useful for tops. Cut off collars and cuffs. Fasten cuffs by hemming and threading with elastic. Remove buttons. Fasten front with Velcro, or other fastening.

LADIES' BLOUSES can also make good tops, particularly blouses with lace. You can use these for boys and girls. Use as they are; do not cut up.

Waistcoats and fitted jackets are suitable too.

CLOAKS (waist length) should hang over the back and one shoulder, leaving sword arm free. Made from almost any material.

OLD TROUSERS make good breeches for Athenian workmen (*A Midsummer Night's Dream*) and others. Cut off trousers below knee. Hem bottom of each leg and thread with elastic.

WOMEN'S SKIRTS can be made to stand away from hips by tying a hoop round the waist.

WOMEN'S TOPS can be made from men's old shirts and fitted by sewing darts.

SHOES should be plain coloured.

Stage fighting

● ● ● ● ● ●

You cannot *improvise* stage fights. That is, you cannot make them up as you go along. Every move must be known in advance and learned in the same way as a dance routine.

Punches and kicks must be faked but must be made to look real. Make the sound of a blow either by slapping hands or, if you are the attacker, by punching your own chest with your free hand. Reactions, grunts and groans help make the fight appear realistic.

For a stage throttle, place your hands outspread on your victim's shoulders with the thumbs against the collarbone. The victim grasps your wrists and makes all the moves. Take special care to make sure that the thumbs only touch on the bone and not higher up: *never* press hard.

'The better part of valour is discretion.' (Henry IV, Part I)

Hairpulling on stage looks quite spectacular though the hair is never actually pulled. Clench your fist and place it on the victim's head. The victim takes tight hold of your wrist with both hands. You are then dragged about by the victim, and not the other way round.

Slaps to the face never connect: the hand travels past the face. You can make the noise of the slap in several different ways. If you are the attacker, slap your other hand, which should be near the victim's face. If you are the victim, clap hands in time with the slap and jerk your head in the same direction as the slap, giving a suitable cry of pain.

You don't actually strike a blow when you give a stomach punch. You hold back your punch, and the victim grabs your fist and pulls it into his/her stomach while doubling over and grunting.

The most spectacular of all the attacks is the kick to the crotch. The kick actually lands on the fleshy inside part of the thigh and is delivered with the inside of the foot and *not* the toe. The victim must remember to stand facing the attacker with legs slightly apart.

'If you have tears, prepare to shed them now.' (Julius Caesar)

Making props

● ● ● ● ● ●

'Props' (short for properties) is the name given to objects which are used by actors on stage. Here are some ideas to help you make some useful props.

TREE TRUNKS

With masking tape, stick two or three large cake or biscuit tins together. You can also use corrugated card or cardboard boxes. Cover them with papier mâché and paint this brown. Break some DIY cork tiles into irregular pieces and stick these on to the dry papier mâché with strong glue.

BACKCLOTH OR HANGING

Suspend a net (garden plastic netting works well). Weave into it pieces of rolled tissue paper (green and brown) and attach leaves made from paper or material. Make paper flowers to add to the collage. Alternatively, lay the netting over large sheets of tissue paper. Stick paper leaves *over* the netting and on to the tissue paper (behind) with white glue.

LARGE LEAVES

Bend thin wire into the outline of a large leaf and its veins. Paste two or three layers of green tissue paper over the structure and allow to dry. Wallpaper paste is best for this.

MORRIS STICKS FOR COUNTRY DANCING

A broom handle, cut in two and taped at each end to stop splinters, will make two Morris sticks.

PARCHMENT SCROLLS

Paint a piece of cartridge paper with a solution of black coffee. When it is dry, crumple it in your hands. Spread it out again and then glue each end of the paper onto round sticks of wood.

FACELESS MASKS FOR WITCHES

Cut an oval shape, just larger than a face, from thick cardboard. Paint one side. When it is dry, glue small, broken bits of polystyrene onto the surface. Paint these too. This gives a strange texture to the mask. Attach a garden cane, or similar, to the back for holding in front of the face.

BREASTPLATE AND SWORD

Cut the front and back from thin card. Join them at the shoulder with thin strips of card. Paint silver. Cut two pieces of card in the shape of a sword. Glue them together with a thin stick inside. Paint silver.

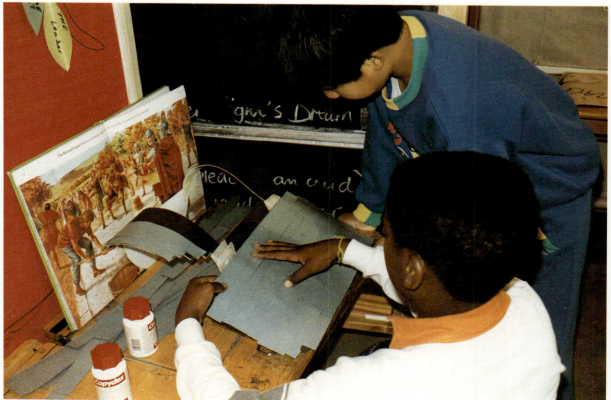

CROWD NOISE

Tape-record a number of people shouting different things. On a second tape recorder, tape the playback together with more live shouting. Keep doing this until it sounds like a large crowd.

FAIRIES' COSTUMES

Old tights and T-shirts can be tie-dyed, or painted, for a dappled forest effect. Stick or sew on home-made leaves and flowers, if wished.

'The rest is silence.' (Hamlet)

Theatrical make-up ('Slap')

● ● ● ● ● ● ●

WHY USE MAKE-UP?

People use make-up in theatrical performances to highlight the features of their faces, so that they can be seen from a distance. Without make-up, faces can look quite blank, especially under stage lighting. People also use make-up to change their age or character. Make-up can also, like masks and costumes, help get rid of shyness.

TYPES OF MAKE-UP

There are basically two types of make-up which are used on stage: 'greasepaint', which Ludwig Leichner invented in 1865, and the more modern, water-based cake make-up.

GREASEPAINT AND HOW TO USE IT

GREASEPAINT usually comes in tubes, pots, or sticks like large crayons. It is waterproof and is available in many different shades and colours. Two of the best known suppliers of theatrical greasepaint are Leichner and Kryolan. Leichner produce thicker sticks, called Form C Standard Sticks, used mainly for foundation, and thinner ones, called Form G Liners. Kryolan make a greasepaint called Supracolor, which can be bought in pots, or in palettes similar to ordinary paintboxes.

Greasepaint is very simple to use. First of all, cover your face and neck with a basic 'foundation' colour. Rub this on the skin and blend it in with your fingers. Put other colours on over the foundation either with your fingers or with a brush. Use liners for shading and highlighting eyes and lips, or for more intricate facial designs.

After you have put on greasepaint, you must 'set' or 'fix' it to prevent it smearing or running. To do this, dab your face with a powder puff dipped in a blending powder. A 150 gram pot of Theatrical Blending Powder is not expensive and will last a very long time.

To remove greasepaint, use a cream such as Crowe's Cremine, Leichner Removing Cream, or ordinary cheap make-up removal cream from any high-street chemist. Work some cream into the greasepaint until the face is covered with a gooey mess. Gently wipe this off with tissues, or with soft toilet paper which is cheaper and just as good.

CAKE MAKE-UP AND HOW TO USE IT

CAKE MAKE-UP is a solid, non-greasy cake of make-up which comes in a small, shallow dish. Both Leichner and Kryolan produce theatrical cake make-up, but ordinary cake make-up, made by cosmetic firms and on sale in any chemist, is just as good. Kryolan's creamy cake make-up is known as 'Aquacolor': you can buy it in palettes containing a dozen or more colours.

This make-up is water-based, and should be put on with a damp piece of sponge. It is an ideal foundation, it spreads more evenly than greasepaint and does not need powdering.

To remove cake make-up, simply wash it off with soap and water.

'. . . to hold, as 'twere, the mirror up to nature.' (Hamlet)

A BEGINNER'S MAKE-UP KIT

You may need a lot of colours in your make-up kit, and it is expensive to buy a large number of sticks, pots and cakes of make-up. However, you only use a small amount of make-up at a time, so it lasts a very long time. If you're starting off, a kit based around one of the palettes with a number of colours could contain the following in it:

General foundation Aquacolor No. 3W (for girls) or No. 5W (for boys)

Small sponge (for foundation)

Pot of Theatrical Blending Powder

Powder puff

Kryolan palette:
- water-based Aquacolor Code B (12 colours)
- grease-based Supracolor Code B (12 colours)

No. 2 brush (to go with palette)

¼ inch brush (to go with palette)

Pot of make-up removing cream

Eyeliners or pencils as required

BASIC TIPS

Boys
- The basic foundation shade for boys is a medium brown or light tan (for example, Aquacolor No. 5W). Black or Asian faces need no foundation: it is more important to stop the face shining by using the blending powder.
- Cheekbones and lips need a slightly reddish touch. Brick red is the most suitable colour, but there are many alternatives.
- Eyes can be lined with various shades of brown, grey or blue.

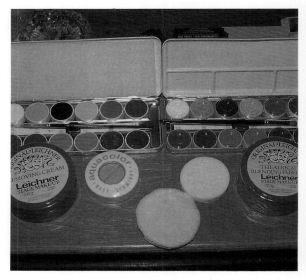

Girls
- Girls usually use a pinky brown or light peach foundation (for example, Aquacolor No. 3W). Again, black or Asian faces need no foundation.
- Eyes can be lined and shaded in a variety of different colours.

To look older
- A paler foundation shade is needed.
- More lines must be drawn on the face.

You need a lot of care and practice to apply stage make-up. As you get better at it, you can add colours to achieve more complicated results. This doesn't need to be expensive: for instance, you can buy eyebrow pencils, which you can use both on greasepaint and cake make-up, very cheaply from most chemists and chain stores.

POINTS TO REMEMBER

1 If you put make-up on too carelessly or too thickly it will look worse than having no make-up on at all. You must set enough time aside to do it properly, and not rush it.

'I will do anything, Nerissa, ere I will be married to a sponge.' (The Merchant of Venice)

2 You must put the foundation colour on evenly. It must cover the whole face, neck and chin. Make sure you don't leave a gap between make-up and costume.

3 Make up your eyes, lips, cheeks, etc. after you've applied the foundation.

4 Shade the face by using colours in hollows. Draw lines along creases in the face with liners or pencils.

SOME SPECIAL EFFECTS

Beards and false hair
Artificial hair is called 'crepe hair' (short ropes of wool plaited with pieces of string) and comes in many different shades.

Pull and stretch out the wool so that you can cut the string off the piece that is to be used. Then comb the wool until the strands separate.

Cut off the amount needed and stick it onto the face with a special glue called 'spirit gum'; you can buy this from shops which

stock theatrical make-up. But be careful: it is dangerous to use any other glue.

Brush a little gum onto the skin and press the hair into place. Trim the hair when it is fixed. Always stick on false hair before you apply make-up.

To remove false hair, soak a little cotton wool in surgical spirit (available from most chemists) and dab it on the face. The hair will gradually come off.

Nose putty
Nose putty is a theatrical modelling clay which you use to make false noses, wounds, warts and other facial alterations.

Knead a piece of nose putty until it is soft, and shape it, making the edges as thin as possible.

Brush a little spirit gum onto the face and attach a few strands of crepe hair. This forms a base.

Press the nose putty onto the hair. Smooth the edges into the skin with make-up removing cream and lightly powder the shape. Now make up the putty with the rest of the face.

To remove nose putty, use surgical spirit and cotton wool as above.

Tooth varnish
You use tooth varnish to make your teeth look as if they are broken or missing. The most common colours are black and white. Be careful: use only theatrical tooth varnish – others can be dangerous.

Blot the tooth dry with a tissue and paint on the varnish. It dries in seconds.

To remove tooth varnish, simply brush the teeth.

'False face must hide what the false heart doth know.' (Macbeth)

It will take a long time to achieve the right effect with make-up. Like most things, it takes practice to be successful at it, but it can be fun to experiment. You can probably buy everything you need from a local Fancy Dress shop: these often stock theatrical make-up, and they should be listed in the Yellow Pages.

In addition, you can visit, telephone or write to the following for information, catalogues and advice:

> Charles H. Fox Ltd
> 22 Tavistock Street
> Covent Garden
> London WC2E 7PY
> (Tel: 071-240-3111)

(Fox's carries a huge stock of theatrical make-up of all kinds and will deliver to all parts of the UK:)

You can also buy make-up, costumes and many other theatrical requirements from:

> Theatre Zoo
> 21 Earlham Street
> Cambridge Circus
> London WC2H 9LL
> (Tel: 071-836-3150)

Leichner have produced charts for detailed character make-up. These charts ('Young Woman', 'Middle-aged Man', 'Clown', etc.) are diagrams which show which colours to use.

There are many make-up books on the market, but most are fairly expensive. However, one of the best is also one of the cheapest: *Make-up Art* by Ron Freeman gives a good introduction to make-up techniques.

'(Exit, pursued by a bear.)' (stage direction in The Winter's Tale*)*